THE TREASURES
OF THE HUNGARIAN
NATIONAL MUSEUM

OLD TEXTILES

MÁRIA VARJÚ-EMBER

OLD TEXTILES

CORVINA KIADÓ · MAGYAR HELIKON

Editor of the Series: Ferenc Fülep,
Director of the Hungarian National Museum, Budapest

Original title: Régi textíliák
Magyar Helikon · Corvina Kiadó, Budapest, 1980
Translated from the Hungarian by Veronica Garami-Burger
Translation revised by Elisabeth West
© Mária Varjú-Ember, 1980
ISBN 963 13 0827 8 · ISBN 963 207 681 8
Photographs by Kálmán Kónya
Colour plates by Egon Gottl
Design by László Ginács
Printed in Hungary, 1981
Kner Printing House, Dürer Workshop, Békéscsaba

INTRODUCTION

In 1857, a modest book was published in Pest with a steel-engraving of the Hungarian National Museum on its cover. Its title was *A Magyar Nemzeti Múzeum. Útmutató ennek műkincsgyűjteményében* (The Hungarian National Museum. A Guide to the Museum's Art Treasures).

What was written in that introduction then is still valid today: "In our days museums no longer represent merely one but rather every aspect of the arts and sciences. Museum objects have their own individual value as unique treasures of art, but they also serve to instruct the viewers. Thus, it can be said that although in times past famous collections were made merely in order to display the magnificence of the chosen objects, today these same objects often help to educate us.

Today a museum must aim at demonstrating those endeavours of the past which belong in the annals of our artistic and scientific pursuits. A national museum should be a treasure-house of a nation's intellectual achievements in particular, and those of mankind in general. It must contain the best of every nation's spiritual, historical, artistic and industrial output. It must stand as a monument to the great minds of the world."

The discussion of textiles occupies only a very small portion of that little book, although the Hungarian National Museum already possessed a collection of costumes and embroideries at that time. In the chapter entitled "Collection of Antiquities", we read: "Furthermore we find here a tall glass cabinet filled with a selection of old Hungarian apparel: foot-wear, hats, embroidered head-dresses, etc. belonging to well-known ladies and gentlemen of the nobility."

It was in the 1920s and 1930s that the museum began to collect textiles in earnest. Embroideries, lace, costumes and other apparel were acquired and exhibited. These acquisitions were made by Elemér Varjú and József Höllrigl. What we know today about the history of costumes we owe largely to Varjú's writings which display his extensive knowledge of both art and history. To Höllrigl we are indebted for his collecting activities and his research, as well as for the opening of the 16th century crypt at Csenger.

During the Second World War the textile collection suffered great losses. After 1945, however, these losses were made good and the collection was enlarged by both acquisitions and donations. The number of pieces rose from five hundred to more than ten thousand. These objects stand as eloquent witnesses to Hungary's memorable history, culture and craftsmanship. They give us an insight into the distant and the more recent past, and the way of life of those who lived before us.

The most valuable textiles are in the permanent collection. Others can be seen during special exhibitions. In 1952 the museum celebrated its one hundred and fiftieth anniversary with a small costume exhibition. In 1957 the main hall of the museum was used for an exhibition entitled: "Treasures in Costumes", where almost one hundred articles of clothing were displayed. In 1962, once more in the main hall of the museum, Hungarian ceremonial dresses were shown. Later that year we were able to see embroideries of the 17th and 18th centuries, with their typical mixture of Renaissance and Turkish motifs. In 1970 there was an exhibition entitled "From Baroque to Art Nouveau". On this occasion furniture was added to enrich a historical survey of costumes, accessories, embroideries, lace, and smaller objects used on either festive or everyday occasions. Textiles always form an important part of the museum's temporary exhibitions of a historical nature, or when new acquisitions are first exhibited.

THE ART OF TEXTILE IN THE MIDDLE AGES AND THE RENAISSANCE

During the 11th century, in Hungary, as in other European countries, Byzantine, Italian and Sicilian silk fabrics were used for ceremonial robes and ecclesiastical vestments. The demand for these fabrics was dictated by the contemporary taste in fashion. Although the earliest Hungarian chasuble has not survived (it was destroyed towards the end of the 18th century) we know something about it from records in the museum's archives. It was made of red Byzantine silk brocade, the figural design was embroidered in Hungary and, according to an inscription, was presented around 1004 by St. Stephen, Hungary's first king and his queen, Gisela, as a gift to Pope John XIX.

The earliest surviving textile of superb quality in the museum's collection is a magnificent coronation robe. Originally it was a chasuble made for the Basilica of Székesfehérvár. It was King Stephen who endowed this church with its furnishings and decorations. From the *Legenda Maior Sancti Stephani Regis* we have the following reference to the vestment: *"Quam qui vidit testimonium veritati verborum nostrorum perhibet innumerabilis palliorum, paramentorum, et aliorum ornamentorum ibi esse genere"* (He who has seen this may bear witness to the truth of our words. Innumerable are the mantles, ecclesiastic vestments and other ornamental things here). It seems therefore that the Basilica owned a great many church vestments. From this rich collection only one chasuble remains, the one donated by the royal couple in 1031. In the 12th century the chasuble was made into a coronation robe. Semicircular in shape, it is 1.343 metres long and 2.685 metres wide. The material is silk patterned with four-petalled rosettes and it is lavishly embroidered with gold thread. In all likelihood, the embroidery was made in the royal workshops founded by Queen Gisela, and the embroiderers were from Regensburg. For many centuries the chasuble must have been an object of great reverence, otherwise the fabric could not have survived. Embroideries from other robes dating from the 12th century were long ago transferred to more recently woven materials.

The focal point of the decoration on the coronation robe is the figure of Christ. Prophets, apostles and saints surrounded by an architectural framework and plant motifs cover the three semicircular panels. In the middle of the lower border the figure of St. Emeric can be seen. On his right and left are the half-figures of Queen Gisela and St. Stephen. The embroidered legend tells us that: ANNO INCARNACIONIS XP (IST) I MXXXI INDICCIONE XIIII A STEPHANO REGE ET GISLA REGINA CASVLA HEC OPERA (T)A ET DA(T)A ECCLESIE SANCTAE MARIAE SITAE IN CIVITATE ALBA (This chasuble was made in the year 1031 of Christ's incarnation and of the 14th indiction by order of King Stephen and Queen Gisela who donated it to the Church of St. Mary in the town of Fehérvár). The embroidery shows direct Byzantine influence together with Carolingian stylistic traditions. The technical execution of the design also brings to mind miniatures made in Regensburg. The decorative composition and the choice of motifs reflect the goldsmith's art, which leads one to believe that a goldsmith may in fact have designed it. Since in 1031 there was war between Hungary and imperial Germany, it may be assumed that the robe was made in Hungary.

Very few of the magnificent treasures which used to belong to the medieval kings of Hungary have survived. In the treasury of Zagreb cathedral there is a chasuble fashioned from a robe belonging to St. Ladislas (1077–1095), king of Hungary. It is made of dark blue Saracen silk decorated with geometrical patterns. The crowned figures in appliqued embroidery and the inscription with the name of St. Ladislas were added at a later date. The paucity of ancient textiles can be attributed to various causes, to continuous warfare on the one hand, and to royal donations to churches abroad (Aachen, Mariazell) on the other. Also, when Hungarian princesses married outside the country, they took their rich dowries with them. At the same time, queens of foreign origin, when widowed, returned to their native countries with many valuable articles from the royal treasury. After her husband's death in 1301, Agnes, the wife of Andrew III, deposited many valuable objects in the cloister of Königsfelden. The queen's last testament informs us that there were a great number of church vestments among these treasures. One of them was a chasuble made from cloth of gold. In the centre of the orphrey the coat of arms of Hungary is embroidered in pearls and encircled by an inscription. A century later Elizabeth, the wife of Albert of Habsburg, King of Hungary (1437–1439), and daughter of Sigismund of Luxembourg (1387–1437), King of Hungary and Holy Roman Emperor (1411–1437), also took many treasures out of Hungary. After the fateful battle of Mohács (1526) the widow of Louis II, Mary of Habsburg, sent to Vienna barge-loads of treasures, among which there were numerous textiles.

Even during the reign of the House of Árpád, Hungarian kings were already importing many splendid woven fabrics from Italy. Three inventories survive from the first half of the 14th century with lists of ecclesiastical vestments from the towns of Veszprém, Pozsony and Kolozsmonostor. According to these inventories the damasks and brocades came from Venice and Lucca. Several were of scarlet silk with plant, animal and other figural motifs such as angels, birds, lions and dogs woven into the fabric.

Hungarian kings and magnates often bought, received or offered as gifts fine Italian textiles. In 1376, for example, the voivode of Transylvania, István Lackfi of Csáktornya, on his return from the Holy Land, received a pillow and a splendidly woven cloth from the Venetian Republic as a token of its esteem. These gifts were originally intended for the Pope. In 1448 Alfonso, King of Naples, sent a fine horse and a richly decorated horse blanket to Governor János Hunyadi. During the reign of King Matthias Corvinus (1458–1490) it was customary to offer woven fabrics as gifts. For example, for his bravery and faithful service, one Bertalan Drágffy received from this king a hanging of cloth of gold.

The 15th century saw the arrival in Hungary of many Italian, especially Florentine, tradesmen, some of whom settled in Buda, where weavers also set up their workshops. In 1486 Beatrice of Aragon, the wife of King Matthias, asked her sister, the Duchess of Ferrara, to send her a silk-weaver master. Three years later, in 1489, the master-weaver Simonello set up trade in Buda.

Some of the embroidery work decorating textiles were made in Hungary by local craftsmen. As a result of royal inter-marriages the creations of these craftsmen found their way into foreign countries from very early times. We find them in Spain, for example. Mary, the daughter of Stephen V, King of Hungary (1270–1272), and the wife of Charles II of Anjou (1285–1309), spent some time in Naples. Their daughter Blanche married Jaime II, King of Aragon (1291–1327). A royal wardrobe inventory in Madrid, dating from 1302, mentions a silk shirt embroidered in the Hungarian fashion *(ad punctum de Ungaria)* with gold, silk and black threads and pearls.

In the 14th century many ornate church vestments were made in the Clarales nunnery in Óbuda. This nunnery was founded in 1334 by Elizabeth, wife of King Charles Robert, and their son Louis the Great. On the occasion of the queen's pilgrimage to Rome she took many beautiful altar cloths and chasubles for the St. Peter Cathedral, all made by the nuns under her supervision. Among the gifts was a violet coloured hanging with figural embroidery. It showed the figures of Patrona Hungariae, St. Peter, St. Paul, St. Louis and the Hungarian saints—Stephen, Emeric, Ladislas, Elizabeth and Margaret. This hanging was mentioned in the Cathedral inventory for the year 1446.

By the 14th century, Hungary had her own master-embroiderers, whose artistic handiwork was universally admired. Between 1384 and 1417 the Dukes of Burgundy employed a Hungarian embroiderer by the name of Etienne le Hongre whose activities are documented from 1373 until 1419.

The 14th century was the Golden Age for the art of embroidery. During the second half of the 15th century there was a decline in the quality of embroidery for churches, with the exception of what is known as raised work. The standard of Italian needlework, on the other hand, remained high.

The conception of a picture to be executed in embroidery demanded a rich and subtle shading of colours. This was achieved by the use of two different methods: *needle painting* (long and short stitch) and the *or nué* technique. The purpose of needle painting, as the name implies, is to create the illusion of painting. This was done by the intricate shading of polychrome silk threads closely stitched together. *Or nué* technique was worked with closely spaced gold cords laid down horizontally from one end of the design to the other. These cords were then bound down by coloured silk threads with alternating loose and close stitches. Thus, a fine three-dimensional *chiaroscuro* effect was achieved. Frequently, the design appeared on a ground cloth made with the above technique in gold embroidery. This technique had already been used in the 4th century and became popular in the 11th and 12th centuries. In order to produce an even more brilliant effect, thin cords were laid under the gold threads following the shape of the pattern. The gold thread was then closely stitched to the cord.

The embroidered ornamentation of cross-shaped orphreys (richly embroidered decorative bands) on ecclesiastical vestments falls into various categories. One of these categories is the representation of biblical scenes with several figures in square-shaped fields. There are two chasubles of this type in the Hungarian National Museum. One depicts scenes from the sufferings of Christ, the other shows the Death of the Virgin. Both vestments date from the beginning of the 15th century.

Designs showing the Crucifixion are also common. On these chasubles the orphrey is entirely filled in by the figure of the crucified Christ with the Virgin, St. John, and Mary Magdalene at his feet *(Fig. 6)*. In later periods the figures appear in an architectural framework. They are placed, for instance, in ogival or domed niches *(Plate I* and *Figs. 1–4)*. In the Late Middle Ages the three-dimensional character of embroidery became more and more pronounced. The figures were in high relief and were enclosed in niches with Romanesque or Gothic arches and pillars *(Plate II* and *Figs. 10–12)*. At the beginning of the 16th century embroidered decorations were placed once again on the ground cloth rather than on the orphrey. The Virgin, often surrounded by a glory of rays, seems to float among the figures of the saints *(Fig. 9)*.

Designs for embroideries on ecclesiastical vestments were often drawn by well-known artists. On the chasuble of Archbishop Tamás Bakócz, one of the treasures of the Esztergom cathedral, the design was made by Pintorucchio. Another chasuble, in the Brukenthal Museum in Sibiu, Rumania, has an embroidered orphrey showing the Trinity. It has been established that the design was made after a drawing by Botticelli. Another of Botticelli's drawings is represented by the Annunciation scene on a chasuble in the collection of the Hungarian National Museum *(Fig. 16)*. Two of Botticelli's *Annunciations* especially come to mind: one in the Uffizi Gallery in Florence, the other in the Glasgow Art Gallery. Another example of great masters' works being imitated is on a chasuble which came to the museum from Sztropkó. Here the embroidered scenes are almost identical in design, composition, and colour scheme with Rogier van der Weyden's triptych painted between 1443 and 1448 *(Plate II and Figs. 11–12)*. This triptych is in the chapel of the hospice at Beaune in France. Though the two artists were separated by distance as well as the space of several decades, there is in the creation of the Hungarian embroiderer a remarkable manifestation of the suggestive power of Rogier's work.

In 1864, in the sacristy of the church in Tököl, Flóris Rómer well known archaeologist discovered ecclesiastical vestments belonging to Frederick III, King of Germany and later Holy Roman Emperor (1440–1493). Of these most noteworthy is a pluvial *(Figs. 7–8)*. It is made of blue velvet and is decorated with embroidered wheat sheaves. On the lower edge of the robe the letters AEIOV and the date 1448 can be seen. The letters are the abbreviation of Frederick III's motto: *Austriae Est Imperare Orbi Vniverso*. The embroidery on his shield shows the Annunciation with figures surmounted by a motto. The most remarkable features are the eared pattern and the aureole-shaped collar on the Virgin's robe. The letters and the date, which also appear on the shield, tell us when the garment was made. It is of German workmanship since the wheat-eared pattern on the Virgin's robe was widely used by German craftsmen.

HAND-WOVEN TEXTILES

The art of weaving developed in Hungary towards the end of the 14th century. King Sigismund recognized its importance and wanted to centralize the craft in the town of Kassa. During the 15th century linen stuffs were woven with an apricot-stone design and decorated with coloured cotton threads, usually blue, woven into the fabric. The pattern of these altar-cloths was worked by starting in the middle and working towards the edges of the cloth. We learn about this method of weaving from the regulations of the fustian weavers' guild of Kassa, dated 1461: "The journeyman who, upon returning from his travels, knows how to do twill weaving may create bird designs, if he so wishes." In 1481 the town council of Kassa forbade the weavers to use twill weaving or to ornament linen with coloured cotton threads. We hear again of the existence of such a piece of cloth in an inventory dated 1553 from the abbey of Zalavár, a "large linen altar-cloth woven at both ends with black and blue threads".

Among the conventional designs used for this type of cloth we find variations of the rosette and star pattern, animals, often in pairs, placed amid floral ornamentation, and in the narrower strips birds and stylized inscriptions. Human figures are also introduced set in an architectural framework of Gothic arches and corbels.

Woven patterns of rosettes, stars and birds are still found today on hand-woven textiles made by peasant craftsmen. Formerly, these were not valued. However, a few of them have been saved for posterity by Kornél Divald and Viktor Miskovszky who rescued them from objects discarded by churches *(Figs. 18, 19)*.

The Dossal of King Mattthias's Throne

Of all our textile treasures the dossal, or hanging of King Matthias's throne is perhaps one of the most significant masterpieces of the Italian Renaissance *(Fig. 20)*. The clearly defined composition is well suited to its size. A 32 cm border surrounds a field which is 106 cm wide and 252 cm long. The design on the lower part of the field represents an ornamental vase standing on the diamond-shaped tiles of a marble floor. The body of the vase is large, spherical in shape, and is covered with a double row in fish-scale pattern. The widest point of the circumference is further emphasized by rows of leaves. The neck has notched decoration. The vase is piled high with pomegranates. On either side cornucopias issue from a bouquet of leaves, pomegranates and pears. The space between the dish and the cornucopias is ingeniously filled with sprays of pomegranate blossom and leaves. On either side of the dish eagles stand poised for flight. The ruffled feathers on the necks and heads are sharply drawn. A pointed tongue darts from each powerful, pointed beak. One third of the dossal's field is occupied by a wreath of oak-leaves among which pears, medlars and pomegranates are placed in alternating sequence. The wreath is held together by bands at the top and at the bottom, while the sides are bound by a braided ribbon ending in tassels. From below the ribbon a pair of cornucopias and rose-sprays issue on either side. Where these meet there is another vase, smaller but similar in shape and design to the one below.

The wreath encloses a shield with the royal arms of King Matthias. In the centre of this shield is an escutcheon with the emblem of the Hunyadi family. The shield is divided into four quarters: in the upper (or chief) part is impaled the coat of arms of Hungary; in the upper left-hand quarter are four silver bars in a red field; in the upper right-hand quarter is a triple mound surmounted by a silver double cross. In the lower half (or base) in an azure field the arms of Dalmatia with three lion heads can be seen, and in a silver field the arms of Bohemia are represented by a red lion. The escutcheon is emblazoned with a black raven perched on a branch in a gold field and holding in its beak a diamond ring. The arched rim of the crown is decorated with fleur-de-lis and the two ends partially cover the shield. The circlet is encrusted with blue, red and yellow gems.

The border of the dossal is divided into three sections—a broad frame enclosed between narrow inner and outer borders. Each narrow border shows a branch entwined with rose leaves. The upper part of the central border ends where it meets with the frame, but the lower part cuts across it, thus creating an impression of firmness and balance. The centre of the upper and lower border is occupied by a leaved wreath on a double-wing, a cornucopia filled with pomegranates and pears issuing to the right and left. This design, cut in half, is repeated eight times in each of the vertical sections of the border. At the base of every other cornucopia, three ears of wheat fill the intervening space. The ground fabric of the dossal is cloth of gold. The design, set into the ground with gold loop weave, is outlined in green velvet. The field and the upper and lower borders are woven as one continuous piece, but the two side borders were woven separately and then sewed together. Possibly the custom was to weave several border strips on one frame which were then cut apart. What seems to support this theory is the fact that on the right-hand border, which has survived in its original condition, there is no evidence of salvage, while on the left, more than half the border has been cut off.

This dossal is a masterly work of art in its overall conception, arrangement of design, and technical execution, and it is a splendid example of the art of weaving in the Renaissance. It reflects the style of an era which favoured, above all, symmetry and balance. The distribution of motifs, the harmonious and graceful arrangement of each decorative element, and the lightness of seemingly cumbersome details, all speak of the genius of the master weaver. It shows the designer's perfect awareness both of the possibilities as well as the limitations of his medium.

The products of Florentine weavers enjoyed great popularity abroad, and their cloths of gold were especially sought after. Among these the most valuable were the so-called Pollaiuolo brocades. On these the patterns were outlined in velvet and filled with looped silver-gilt thread on a flat gold ground.

The Florentine weavers created unique pieces made to order, based on drawings. Apart from the throne dossal, few such pieces have survived. We know of only three altar frontals, one of which was commissioned by Pope Sixtus IV, who in 1475 donated it to the church of S. Francesco in Assisi. In the centre of the broad brocade band stands the figure of St. Francis, and before him, the kneeling figure of the donor. On the two sides, enclosed in oak-wreaths, is the arms of the Rovere family with the inscription: *Sixtus IIII. Pont. Maximus.* The field has a scatter design of capriciously curving oak branches issuing from the wreaths. The border design consists of leafy branches. There is a less elaborate design on the altar frontal in Toledo Cathedral. This bears the arms of Cardinal Pedro Gonzales de Mendoza (d. 1495). The ground is densely covered with foliage and thistle flowers. The wreath of fruits laced in four places by ribbons which surrounds the coat of arms is in the style and spirit of the Renaissance. A double shield with the armorial bearings of Lodovico il Moro and Beatrice d'Este, who were married in 1491, decorates the altar frontal in Varese (Museo di Santa Maria del Monte). Laurel leaves and olive branches enclose the shields.

The weaving of all three altar frontals is identical with that of the throne dossal. Even the designs show similarities. The oak leaves on the Assisi brocade, the pomegranates on the Toledo brocade, the ribbons binding the wreaths on both, and the finely drawn foliage of the Varese brocade, all show a striking resemblance to the ornamentation of the dossal. Other examples are the pluvial of Henry VII, King of England (1485–1509), now in Stonyhurst College, and the rose-patterned brocade in the Metropolitan Museum in New York. The fact that all these brocades were made between 1470 and 1500 is evidenced by Henry's will which mentions that the pluvial came from Florence.

The dossal is a rare example of "made to order" textiles. Although unique in the perfection of its decorative composition, some of the pattern details may be encountered elsewhere. In the treasury of the cathedral at Esztergom there is a brocade chasuble of Florentine workmanship dating from around 1470. While the technical execution is identical with that of the dossal, some of the design motifs are similar to those of the throne hanging. For instance, the cornucopia filled with pomegranates and the ears of wheat appear on both. Similar patterns appear on a dalmatic, made of Florentine silk brocade, now in the Geistliche Schatzkammer in Vienna. The wreaths on a ground of feathers, the palmettes and the ribbons are similar to the motifs on the dossal. The flower-entwined branches, and the eagles poised for flight also appear on 15th century Florentine textiles. On a fresco in the church of Santa Maria Novella, painted by Domenico Ghirlandaio in 1490, Giovanni Tornabuoni wears a brocade gown decorated with eagles. Hungary's coat of arms, as it appears on the dossal, also finds its parallel on the so-called Matthias Tower of the Church of Our Lady (Matthias Church) in Buda. This shield in high-relief was cut in 1470 and it is identical with its embroidered counterpart, the only difference being that on the sculpture the circlet of the crown is closed. The coat of arms depicted in the codex of St. Jerome, once in King Matthias's famous Bibliotheca Corviniana, and the coat of arms carved into Matthias's stall (Hungarian National Museum) are also similar to the shield on the dossal.

Pope Sixtus IV's altar frontal, with a design inspired by a drawing of Antonio Pollaiuolo, comes closest in style to the dossal. It, too, was probably based on the same drawing. Furthermore, the eagle motif on the dossal bears a close resemblance to Pollaiuolo's enamelled eagle on a silver cross in the Baptistry in Florence.

As to the dating of the dossal, we gain our information from a Florentine gold brocade hanging, originally in the possession of Charles the Bold, which, after the battle of Grandson in 1476, fell into Swiss hands. It was presumably made at the same time as the dossals, that is, around 1476. The pomegranate and rose motifs on the brocade and the dossal are almost identical. It is mentioned in the inventories of the cathedral of Florence that Pollaiuolo, an artist of many talents, was employed by the Duomo to design the decoration, including the embroidery, for brocades made by the most sophisticated weaving methods. The inventories also mention the name of the designer and maker of the above-mentioned brocades. The similarities between the technical execution of the altar frontal, the gold hanging and the dossal lead one to believe that all three were made in the same workshop. (The weaver of the most beautiful brocades of the period was Francesco Malocchi who worked in close collaboration with members of Pollaiuolo's workshop.)

Another dossal made for the throne of King Matthias, identical in design with the one already mentioned, was later used for making a chasuble *(Plate III)*. This hanging has an interesting history. In 1874 the following lines appeared in the Hungarian bulletin *Archaeologiai Értesítő*: "Recently the Hungarian consul in Belgrade, Mr. Jenő Kállay, a devoted student of the sciences, having made a trip into the mountainous regions of Bosnia on horseback in search of all its places of interest, explored the area's least known corners. Among other things, he discovered to his great delight in the Foynicza convent of Cresovo a 15th century pluvial with the armorial bearings of the Hunyadis..." (This announcement contained several incorrect statements: Kállay's first name was Béni, and the pluvial was in fact a chasuble.)

The chasuble was shown in 1876 at an exhibition organized to benefit the victims of a flood. Arnold Ipolyi, bishop of Nagyvárad, was the first to do research on it, and his findings were published in the monthly review *Századok*. In his attempt to discover whether this magnificent piece of brocade was originally intended for ecclesiastical or secular use, he did not reach a final conclusion, but assumed that it must have been the mantle of a king. He rejected the supposition that the brocade was originally made for ecclesiastical use, since the back panels of chasubles were traditionally ornamented with figures of saints, not the large-size coats of arms of the donor; nor could it have been a king's mantle, since there is no known instance of a king's personal arms having been woven into the fabric of a mantle. At this time, Ipolyi also raised the idea of acquisition: "No one could conceive of a more fitting ceremonial vestment for the coronation of our Hungarian kings. No price should be considered too great to acquire it, so that it may take its rightful place among our coronation regalia."

In 1885 negotiations were opened for the purchase of the chasuble. The abbess of the convent in Fojnica offered it to the Archbishop of Hungary, but the negotiations ran into difficulties. Then, with Béni Kállay as mediator, Franz Joseph I bought it, and the following announcement appeared in the press on 7 February, 1886: "In the convent of Foynicza in Bosnia a valuable chasuble has been preserved. The coat of arms of Hungary, together with the Corvinian arms, appear on its central panel. This chasuble, of great artistic value and historical significance, was presented, in all likelihood, by Matthias, King of Hungary, to Katalin Tomashevitch, Queen of Bosnia. Recently, his Imperial and Apostolic Highness acquired it and graciously presented it to the Hungarian nation on condition that it should serve for ever as the coronation robe of the kings of Hungary, and furthermore, that it should be safely deposited in the royal chapel of Buda Castle."

At the time that the Fojnica chasuble was discovered, the existence of the throne dossal was still unknown. Since historian Vilmos Fraknói had seen a similar brocade in the possession of the Erdődy family in Galgóc, Imre Szalay, ministerial councellor, asked Vilmos Migazzi, the father-in-law of Imre Erdődy, to arrange a viewing of the brocade. In 1887 Migazzi brought the dossal to Budapest and took it to Szalay's apartment. The similarity between the Fojnica chasuble and the dossal was immediately recognized; the only difference was that the dossal bore the coat of arms of Archbishop Tamás Bakócz which, however, was not embroidered on the fabric, but was sewn onto it. When the coat of arms was removed, the escutcheons of Hungary and King Matthias came to light. How the dossal came into the possession of Archbishop Bakócz must remain, in part, congesture. We know that on the death of King Matthias, Queen Beatrice and the king's natural son, János Corvinus, became his heirs. Bakócz helped Corvinus to become the ban of Croatia, and gave him a large loan. In return, János Corvinus pawned many valuable articles to Bakócz, articles which remained in the Archbishop's possession. It must have been at this time that the Archbishop acquired the dossal and had his own coat of arms superimposed on it. Furthermore, the treasury catalogue of the archbishopric of Esztergom, dating from 1553, mentions new articles which came to the cathedral as a bequest from Bakócz, among these two hangings bearing the Bakócz arms, one of gold velvet, the other with raised floral designs on a gold velvet ground. A third hanging, made of cloth of gold, carried the royal arms of Hungary. The treasury inventory of 1609 also includes a hanging with the Bakócz arms, and a cloth of gold hanging with the escutcheons of Hungary and King Matthias. In the middle of the 16th century, there were three escutcheoned hangings in the treasury of Esztergom Cathedral; by 1609, there were only two. It is conceivable that the third hanging had already been converted into a chasuble, and that the Franciscan friars took it to Bosnia. (The above-mentioned statement in the press, that King Matthias gave the chasuble to the Queen of Bosnia, cannot be verified by any reliable document.

However, Archbishop Bakócz was related to the Erdődy family, which could explain how the dossal became the property of the Erdődys.)

There are a number of minor differences on the brocade of the dossal and the chasuble. On the wreath of the dossal the ribbon on top is gold, the rest are silver, while those on the chasuble are all silver; the eyes of the eagle on the dossal are gold, on the chasuble they are blue, and the lower lids are red. The colours of the jewels in the crown on the dossal are blue, red, blue, yellow, red, yellow, red, blue and red. On the chasuble there is only an alternation of red and blue. On the dossal the raven holds a green ring in its beak. On the chasuble the ring is red, with a green circle round it.

There are two brocade fragments in the Hungarian National Museum which, at one time, were part of chasubles. The patterns and the manner of weaving are identical with those of the dossal, the only difference being that on the fragments the patterns are picked out by red velvet contours. These two chasuble fragments were cut from the borders of the dossal. One difference in the weaving is that the ring holding together the two cornucopias is woven with silver threads.

The dossal, the chasuble, and the fragments were made by exactly the same weaving methods. The surviving fabrics seem to prove that King Matthias ordered three dossals for the throne to be woven according to the same specifications. It appears that in each palace where there was a throne, the throne was given its own dossal. There are extant written documents testifying to the sumptuous furnishings of the palace in Buda. Seybold, the German ambassador who attended the king's wedding in 1476, described the banqueting hall thus: "The walls were covered with silk hangings. Above the head of the table a canopy was raised made of cloth of gold on which one could make out the pearl-encrusted arms of both King and Queen." Furthermore, on the front page of the Ransanus codex, written by the Dominican bishop who was King Ferdinand's Neapolitan ambassador at the court of King Matthias, there is a miniature portraying the royal couple seated on their throne. Both the dossal and the underside of the canopy of the throne are made of elaborately decorated brocade fabric.

In the palaces of King Matthias there were a great many woven hangings. It is noteworthy that he chose for the dossal of his throne a hanging made of brocade. His appears to be the only dossal specially woven, measured and designed to order. Its purely Renaissance pattern was unique at the time and pointed the way to future developments in the weaving industry.

The Ceremonial Sword Belt of King Vladislav II

For centuries it was the custom for popes to bless a ceremonial sword and cap which was then presented to a European king, an outstanding member of a dynasty, or a great general. The first such ceremonial sword was presented by Pope Urban V at the Christmas celebrations of 1365 to Louis of Anjou, later King of Naples. This custom survived until 1825.

At first, the blessing and presentation of a sword was either a mark of chivalry or a symbol of gratitude for services rendered. During the papacy of Julius II, the custom also served political expediency. At the Christmas celebrations of 1509 the pope followed his blessing of the sword by announcing to his cardinals that he was going to send it to Vladislav II, King of Hungary (1490–1516). Clearly, his purpose was to win the allegiance of the Hungarian king for the League of Cambrai.

Achille de Grassis and the Bishop of Modrus-Zengg (Modruš Senj) arrived in the town of Tata on 2 July, 1510. The latter carried the sword point upwards, the cap resting on the point. For this reason the ornamentation on both sword and scabbard were upside down.

The sword belt was used in the girding ceremony *(Fig. 21)*. The goldsmith Domenico de Sutri fashioned the blade, while the belt was woven by Bernardo Ser Silvano, who worked for Julius II and made all the brocade belts for the swords given as gifts by the pope.

The belt is made of gold brocade. The design, in which three motifs are repeated, is outlined with red silk. The Rovere arms with its elaborately drawn shield showing an oak tree, roots and acorns also appears on the scabbard. Above the shield the papal tiara can be seen with two crossed keys. The two motifs are connected by a vine bearing oak leaves and acorns. The gold of the fabric is relieved by silver threads covering the space between the three segments of the crown and by the silver of the keys underneath. The shield is woven on a blue silk ground. The belt is faced with gold brocade. 78 cm of the reverse side, where the belt would hang loosely after the girding, is lined with brocade. The remaining length is lined with red silk. The silver-gilt buckle is decorated with Late Gothic leaf motifs. The reinforced openings of the fifteen pairs of buckle tongues are made of silver gilt decorated with three acorns and two leaves.

During his eleven years in office, Pope Julius II (1503–1513) bestowed nine ceremonial swords. The recipients were Philip I the Handsome of Spain (1503); Henry VII of England (1504); Louis XII of France (1505); James IV, King of Scotland (1506); and Charles III, Duke of Savoy (1507). The year 1508 seems to have passed without a recipient. In 1509 Vladislav II, King of Hungary, received the sword; in 1510 the Swiss Confederation (Eidgenossenschaft); and in 1511 Raimondo de Cardona, Viceroy of Naples.

The sword and belt of James IV of Scotland are in Edinburgh in the royal treasury. The Swiss sword is in the Landesmuseum in Zurich. These two swords are almost identical with the sword of Vladislav II. The brocade fabric of the belts is also similar although there is a slight difference in length, while the silk ground of the Rovere shield is not blue but light green.

The history of Vladislav's sword is only partially known. The widow of King Louis II (1516–1526) of Hungary, immediately after the ill-fated battle of Mohács, fled to Pozsony with the treasury. One year later, an inventory was ordered by Emperor Ferdinand. In the following year the emperor and his sister Mary shared out the treasures between them. Ferdinand's son, Archduke Ferdinand, either received the sword as part of his inheritance, or as a gift. Still later, the sword can be traced to the treasury in Vienna. It was handed over to Hungary in 1932. Since then the sword belt has been one of the most valuable objects in the Hungarian National Museum.

HUNGARIAN EMBROIDERY IN THE 16TH AND 17TH CENTURIES

Of all the possible ways of decorating textiles, embroidery is the most diversified. It can be as colourful as a painting, or as plastic as a sculptured relief. Openwork, drawn-thread embroidery can create the illusion of intricate carving. The elaborate and clearly delineated designs embroidered with gold and silver thread remind one of the art of the goldsmith. There are so many types of stitchery, and the plotting is so free, even when the design depends on the counting of threads, that machine-made and decorated textiles are always of an inferior quality to those made by hand.

It may be said, therefore, that of the textiles that can be considered as works of art embroidery fulfils best the intentions of the artist. It provides ample opportunity for expression for both the designer and the embroiderer for their artistic ability and their technical expertise. The embroiderer can select both material and stitches and vary them at will, and he may plot his lines freely. His freedom is unlimited, whereas the weaver's methods are always dictated by the very nature of the art of weaving. For this reason, from among the decorative arts, embroidery became the most suitable expression of the artistic sensitivity of the common folk.

Though during their long evolution the decorative arts in Hungary have absorbed influences from East and West alike, we must not overlook the significant contribution of local tradition in their development. On a sabretache plate (from Bezdéd) dating from the time of the Magyar Conquest around A.D. 900 we find pineapple motifs similar to those on an embroidery made in the 17th century. On another sabretache plate (from Galgóc) decorated with a lattice-work of ribbons, we see acanthus blossoms similar to those in Italian Renaissance ornamentation as well as on Hungarian embroideries of a much later date. The Eastern influence reached Hungary direct from Byzantium during the Middle Ages. Later it arrived indirectly through Italy, particularly through Venice. This influence has survived until our days mainly on stone-carving. The Italian influence reached Hungary in the second half of the 15th century, before penetrating any other European country and during the reign of King Matthias, Italian Renaissance art became firmly rooted in this country. However, during the Turkish occupation Persian and Turkish decorative motifs predominated.

Hungarians have always been acutely sensitive to beauty and innovation. Around the middle of the 16th century, a new style of embroidery evolved which was the product of a happy amalgamation of forms adopted from East and West and of those peculiar to the traditional native taste.

In those days, Hungary occupied a geographical position between the stylistic currents of countries lying to the East and West. Consequently, she received impetus from both sides. Nevertheless it was a deep-rooted native culture, as well as strong individual creative impulse, that made possible the emergence of a typically Hungarian art form which combined and adapted stylistic elements from such widely differing sources. This new and typically Hungarian idiom in the art of embroidery emerged during the most desperate period of the national struggle to drive out the Turkish invaders. In 1526, the fate of Hungary was decided at the disastrous battle of Mohács, and the country was divided into three parts, a division that lasted for 150 years. It was during those years of constant warfare that Hungarian embroiderers perfected a style of embroidery which reflected both Renaissance and Turkish influence. Although the country was politically divided, Hungarians succeeded in maintaining their national identity, a homogeneity of outlook that is reflected in the nation's culture, art, and customs. This explains the development of only one style of embroidery, and is the reason why it is difficult to ascertain today the exact geographical origin of individual undocumented pieces of embroidery.

Hungarian domestic embroidery dating from this period owes its greatest debt to the wealth of Italian Renaissance ornamentation. The creations of Italian artists were free of artificiality; the rhythm is free-flowing and varied, and the lines have a natural grace. The network of vines covering the surfaces, and the decorative motifs introduced to emphasize certain areas, give the total composition a clearly defined structure. The drawings are well proportioned. Where flowers comprise the chief element of ornamentation, the distribution of stems, bushes, branches or vines is beautifully balanced. The vines swell, branch out or run together with a vital rhythm of their own. The embroidered designs are never over-powering, and the sober arrangements show a striving to avoid crowding in the overall impression. The choice of colours, the diversity of stitches, and the judicious use of gold and silver thread further add to the harmony of the whole. Although floral patterns predominate, not all Renaissance decorative elements were adopted in Hungarian embroidery. The vine-leaf motif, so favoured in Italian pattern-books, is relatively rare in Hungarian embroidery, while arabesques are totally absent. The trellis pattern also appears infrequently, and when it does, its shape is changed into knots in figure eight forms. Dragons, griffins, and serpents are replaced by heraldic beasts such as lions, stags and birds. Figural designs are almost exclusively reserved for ecclesiastical embroidery.

The patterns and techniques of English needlework dating from this period are almost identical with those of Hungarian pieces.

Contemporary Russian and Polish embroideries also evidence features in common with Hungarian embroidery.

Hungarian Renaissance embroidery flourished during the 16th and 17th centuries. Extant inventories show that Renaissance embroidery was not adopted exclusively for the ornamentation of textiles made for ceremonial and festive occasions, but that it was regularly used to adorn articles of everyday use. Infants' robes, childrens' dresses, bridal trousseaus, male and female garments, pillows and sheets made for the bier, even the handkerchiefs placed in the hands of the deceased were all embellished with embroidery.

Women's embroidered bodices and shifts are listed in great quantities in inventories. The needle-wrought apron usually matched the decoration on the blouse. The collar and front of men's shirts, the short and wide sleeved dolmans, were all picked out in silver and gold thread. Handkerchiefs are also mentioned in abundance. The women held them in their hands, the men tucked them into their belts or pockets so that the embroidered designs and lace edgings could be displayed to advantage.

The first guild of embroiderers was established in Buda, followed by others in the provinces. In this way, the names of some of the Hungarian craftsmen who worked between the 15th and 17th centuries have come down to us. Gergely Seydenhafter became a citizen of Kassa in 1463. In 1468 he became a member of the town council. Jakab and János were master beadworkers. The former was active in 1471, the latter between 1475 and 1484. Zsigmond Perlhefter worked in Brassó between 1533 and 1534. He was engaged by the church of Besztercebánya in 1545 to work as an *acupictor quidam ex Olmutz* (needle painter of Olmutz). Bona Nyilassi, master embroiderer and beadworker, worked in Eger with his apprentice András. In 1556 he embroidered and beaded garments entrusted to him by the captain. His employer must have been pleased with him, because in the following year he was named "official beadworker for their Highnesses, the princes of Transylvania". In 1640, Jakab the Pouch-Maker, a citizen of Kassa, worked mostly on horse blankets and pouches. There is only one woman's name among the embroiderers, that of Katalin Hímvarró ("the Embroideress") who was active in the middle of the 17th century.

Hungarian journeymen travelled far and wide in Europe, settling here and there to ply their trade for a while before returning home. During the Turkish wars these journeymen constituted the only links between Hungary and countries lying to the north and west.

When they came home, they brought with them embroidery samplers and a knowledge of new fashions in stitchery which they adapted to please local taste. Thus, they, too, contributed to the style of embroidery peculiar to Hungary in the 17th century.

The creations of professional embroiderers display a sound knowledge of drawing and composition. Of all European stylists, they were most influenced by the Renaissance. Despite technical intricacies and tiring procedures, their craftsmanship is of very high quality.

Professional embroiderers and their journeymen adorned the skirts and corset-bodices of women's gala dresses, men's dolmans and short fur-lined coats with silver and gold thread, pearls and coral. They embroidered floral patterns on saddles and horse-blankets, velvet covers, coverlets, curtains and bed hangings. Even the men's boots, the ladies' shoes, and the leather purses attached to belts boasted of embellishments of silver and gold thread. Ecclesiastical vestments especially were profusely embroidered with floral patterns in coloured silks, and threads of gold and silver. The pattern itself was plotted by a pattern-drawer who was guided by the importance, taste, and need of his client. Church account books show that the brocades, velvets, and atlas needed for the making of these vestments were mostly purchased from Italian merchants, but that the sewing and embroidery were done by local craftsmen. The 1692 regulations of the embroiderers' guild of Kassa testify to this when they state: "The young man who wishes to excel in his art must be qualified to embroider coats of arms for the vestments of the nobility and the clergy as well as for the trappings of their horses. Above all must he excel in the stitching of mitre with gold and silver."

In a pattern book from the town of Kisszeben, dating from 1641, we find the picture of a chasuble embroidered with Hungarian Renaissance motifs. In fact, by the middle of the 15th century, Hungarian needle-workers were well acquainted with Italian embroidery patterns. In 1458 an inventory was taken of the estate of the wife of one Johannes Lewkes de Kallo which includes *Vnum culcitrum ad modum ytalicorum* (a shirt made in the Italian fashion).

Master embroiderers also made use of motifs found in German and Venetian pattern books, most of which were published in the 16th century. The Hungarians were inspired partly by the drawings found in these books, and partly by the designs of Italian brocades.

Turco-Persian decorative motifs had already appeared before the Turkish occupation of Hungary. This was the consequence of a treaty made in 1449 which had guaranteed the right of the Turkish merchants to sell their wares at the fairs held in the southern towns of Hungary. It was not long before these merchants made their appearance in Buda where Sigismund, Prince of Poland, the younger brother of the Hungarian king Vladislav II, purchased in 1500 Turkish embroidered stuffs.

It was customary among the Turks to offer textiles, especially embroidered ones, as gifts. Hungarian envoys to Turkey were given kaftans and embroidered scarves. Murat, janissary aga of the Turkish soldiers stationed in Buda, sent such a kerchief in 1560 to István Dobó, the commander of Eger Castle. The gift was accompanied by a letter: "I have sent to your lordship a very beautiful blue *markaman* [kerchief used to store the ceremonial turban] with which it is my hope to please your lordship." In 1607 Bayran bey, when set free from captivity, sent a kerchief as part of his ransom. He wrote: "I am sending a kerchief worthy of your lordship and your lady." Kerchiefs were in great demand when Turkish merchants came to Hungary during the 17th century.

In castles and manors, during the winter months, many hours were given over to sewing and embroidery by the chatelaines and their serving women. They worked according to drawings made beforehand, and often they were instructed by Hungarian or Turkish seamstresses. In this manner the trousseaus were prepared and the linens were embroidered with gold, silver and coloured silks, sometimes even with woollen yarn. Hungarian women, however, learned embroidery not only from professional Turkish seamstresses *(bulya)*, but also from the wives of the Turkish nobility living in Hungary. Many letters testify to the fact that Hungarian and Turkish women often exchanged patterns. Many sought the advice of the wife of Amhat aga, who lived in Fehérvár, and she would reply in Hungarian, including samplers in her letters.

Many different kinds of skilled artisans lived in the castles of the Hungarian nobility. Among these were, of course, the embroiderers and the beadworkers. Turkish seamstresses were also employed. When eventually they were released from captivity, they sent many embroidered stuffs to their former mistresses. In Hungary, they also learned the local patterns and thus, together with Hungarian women captured by the Turks, they contributed to the development of Turkish-Hungarian designs.

When members of the nobility went on their travels, they made sure that their wives who remained at home to look after children, home, and estate, should have competent men and women to do their sewing and embroidery. In 1596 György Thurzó wrote to his wife, "I found a very good Turkish seamstress for my dear wife whom I wish to please in all things". Gábor Bethlen, Prince of Transylvania, wrote to his first wife Zsuzsanna Károlyi in 1621 "My sweet Susan, I hired for your service an embroiderer master who will know how to make for you precious stuffs of velvet and silk. This man has no one to equal him even in Germany." In 1716, after having settled her brothers and sisters, Kata Bethlen engaged a certain János Timár embroiderer master. Later we find a "seamster Bukor" among her staff.

The wives of magnates, women of the lesser nobility and of the middle classes, sewed and decorated every article of clothing for their families. When a more splendid dress was called for, many letters were written and exchanged. The women made and collected patterns and kept them at hand, never knowing when they may need them. These patterns were kept not only in the form of drawings, but were actually made into samplers, and were considered of great value. In 1563 Magdolna Guthy Ország addressed a letter to her daughter in which she complained that friends had borrowed her patterns which they were reluctant to return: "...there is one of considerable value at my Lady Borbála. It is a large old pattern for weaving and beadwork which had been done for your wedding. Therefore, with words gentle or harsh, but do go and fetch it from her. First ask her with civility, unless she will not let you have it. Surely, she must have it. I tell you, we would be less saddened by the loss of some precious treasures than to see that pattern gone from us for good."

The estate book of István Tatay, dated 1607, mentions six embroidered samplers, further proof that in those days such items were highly regarded.

It is regrettable that only one of the samplers and a few of the drawings have come down to us. Of all those once owned by Júlia Rédei, the wife of Miklós Bethlen (1642–1717), Chancellor of Transylvania, only eight drawings are extant today. They can be dated to the second half of the 17th century, and were still in use at a later period. Júlia Rédei was married in 1686. Three of the drawings bear her signature, and two others are signed by her daughter Ágnes Bethlen, who married the nobleman Zsigmond Kemény in 1719.

The name and arms, garlanded by flowers, of Júlia Rédei were embroidered onto an altar-cloth of the Calvinist church in the town of Torda. The garland and the flower motifs are similar to the garland on a cloth in the collection of the Hungarian National Museum *(Figs. 42–43)*. On the museum's sample-drawing No. 6, the sunflower, which has a grill-pattern centre, is surrounded by four serrated leaves. There are three similar embroideries in the museum *(Figs. 38, 39, 40)*. Sample-drawing No. 1 is almost identical with the pattern on an embroidered pillow-slip *(Fig. 22)*, where the distribution of large tulips issuing from an encircling vine, the small flowers filling the spaces, and even the type of stitching, are closely reminiscent of the sample. On three drawings by Júlia Rédei, the slanting flower bushes are similar to the graceful bush designs on the borders of a velvet coverlet worked by the noblewoman Zsuzsanna Lorántffy *(Plates VII–VIII* and *Figs. 57–58)*.

Textiles enriched with embroidery added to the splendour of festive occasions and helped to brighten articles of everyday use. There was a growing tendency to decorate with gold and silver thread and multicoloured silks clothing and household linens of every kind.

In the 17th century embroidery was an indispensable addition to all ceremonial apparel. Whether decorated with silver thread or pearls, these robes were created by masters of the art, and nothing to compare with them has been made since. The skirt of Catherine of Brandenburg, second wife of Gábor Bethlen, Prince of Transylvania, is cut in the Hungarian fashion and is richly decorated with rows of gold and silver flower arcades *(Fig. 54)*. The embroidery on the corset was, of course, worked to match the skirt. Shoes for men and women, gloves and leather purses, women's silk stockings, were all embroidered in gold. Embroidered handkerchiefs were part of a rich person's finery. We see them on portraits of young women who hold them in their hands; and in the hands of noblemen and priests, when depicted lying in state. A bride embroidered her own betrothal kerchief, and at the appropriate time, in exchange for his ring, she sent the groom her own ring tied to the gold-embroidered kerchief.

Handkerchiefs were most often embroidered at the corners. Usually the flower stems point diagonally towards the centre, while occasionally the bouquets start from a centrally placed rosette and are worked toward the corners. Some trousseaus contained as many as twenty-five handkerchiefs adorned with gold, silver and coloured silk threads. Some were sewn in Spanish stitch, others had gold-filled patterns of roses or carnations. Kerchiefs embroidered with Persian and Turkish devices were locally made, the style borrowed from Oriental sources. Wardrobe accounts and bequests give an accurate picture of the sophisticated splendour of the period taste in fashion. By the 16th century it was fashionable to decorate the shirts and blouses of men and women with gold and silver stitches, multi-coloured borders, or a network of gold thread. The woven fabrics were shot with gold, embroidered with red, white or black stitching. These variations were further enriched in the 17th century with drawn-thread work, openwork edgings, flowers made of gold and silver mixed with multicoloured silk yarns, or blossoms of pure silver and gold. The motifs were either Hungarian or borrowed from Turkey, Poland, Italy, Spain and other countries.

Pillow-slips were embroidered either at one narrow end, or else had wide patterned borders on three sides of the upper side. The embroidery at the short end of a pillow-slip usually comprised three borders—a middle band of flower motifs flanked by two narrower bands of garlands or, more often, rows of tiny flowers. The embroidery covering three sides of a full pillow-slip was made up of similar patterns. Pillows made in the 16th century were mostly embroidered in gold and silver, while coloured silks were added in the 17th century. There were also pillow-slips decorated with white thread and openwork.

Wardrobe accounts provide us with a list of useful information. For instance, pillow-slips were often lined with gold taffeta so that the gold, antique white, and rose pink flowers on the openwork outer cover would show to greater advantage. In 1595 pillow-slips made for the two beds owned by one Kata Károlyi were edged with gold lace, a gold spray was embroidered in each corner, and along each side ran a narrow border of embroidery. As a rule, four pillows were made for each bed. The smallest of the four was usually laid on top. A young bride's trousseau also included a mortuary pillow adorned with black embroidery.

The wife of András Ujfalussy, née Éva Károlyi, received a trousseau in which, according to an inventory dated 1670, all her bed linen was decorated with the same designs; each richly embroidered sheet had four matching pillow-slips, and the wide borders with floral designs were picked out in gold.

These profusely decorated sheets were early versions of the blanket-covers used today. They were embroidered at the two narrow ends which were folded back over the blanket. Bedsheets, on the other hand, were embroidered along the long sides which hung over the edge of the bed. The embroidered borders of sheets consisted of separate linen strips which were sewn to the sheet by looped stitches. A frequently occurring motif in these borders consists of leaves arranged in rows either facing each other or pointing in one direction only. The flowers are often tied into a garland by a long vine. The embroidered borders are sometimes attached to all four sides of the sheet, sometimes only to the side which is meant to show. More complex patterns were embroidered directly onto the edge of the sheet.

Kata Károlyi's trousseau inventory of 1595 gives a detailed description of the embroidery on the sheets of this rich landowner's daughter. Two of them were worked in gold and silver thread, a third had a peacock design, and a fourth was trimmed at both ends with network lace depicting the life of Abraham. On others the edges were embroidered with floral motifs incorporating roses and stars. For these designs, sometimes in openwork, white or coloured silks were used. Bands of openwork with white embroidery had borders of drawn threadwork. Another trousseau inventory dating from 1603 lists items belonging to one Zsuzsanna Thurzó. It mentions three sheets each embroidered on three sides with gold, silver and silk thread. This type of decoration seems to have been the most often applied in the 17th century. In 1612 one of the daughters of the Thurzó family was given nineteen such sheets. In 1618 another daughter received twenty-four. By 1630, sheets were embroidered along all four borders. In 1660 the trousseau of Katalin Illésházy included forty-six richly decorated sheets and thirty less ornate ones.

There are several references in inventories to sheets with the "standing" flower stem, named thus after the vertical orientation of the motifs. There are also frequent references to *kamuka* embroidery in which the design was stitched on a silk ground, and the name probably comes from old Turkish or Persian meaning silk damask. (When the embroiderer used threads of the same colour as the silk foundation, he produced an effect resembling damask.) *Shaded embroidery* was the term used to describe white patterns outlined with dark thread.

The edges of sheets were frequently embellished with *network lace*. The net was patterned with coloured floral or figural designs. The figures were usually inspired by biblical subjects: Adam and Eve, the Annunciation, the Sacrifice of Isaac, or St. George the Dragon Slayer. The lace was edged with drawn-work which again had another network border.

In 1674 the Pauline fathers took over the Calvinist church in the town of Nagyszombat. Listed in the church inventory, there is a tablecloth of network lace decorated with the figures of Abraham and Isaac.

Sheets decorated with cutwork show the typical Hungarian Renaissance motifs over the square mesh foundation. Edges are finished with drawn-thread embroidery and bobbin lace.

The making of bed linen was everywhere a domestic art. Silk hangings and velvet coverlets were entrusted to the professional embroiderer, who embellished them with gold and silver thread. Canopied beds were given hangings called *superlát*. Even mirrors were draped with curtains which could be pulled aside or drawn at will. At a time when furniture tended to be dark and heavy, gay embroidered draperies lent an air of friendliness to rooms. Reds, greens, purples and grays were used in all their variations. Shades of red varied between cardinal, scarlet, flame, brick and coral; among the greens were hues of olive, grass and sea; and purples came in shades of violet, lavender, lilac, puce and mauve. There were also dove-grays, ash-grays, and pearl-grays. Against a shimmering atlas background silver and gold thread was used to emphasize the forms of embroidered flowers. When noblemen went on long journeys they took their own bed linen and hangings with them. Count Imre Thököly took into exile his own *superlát* of gold-embroidered red satin.

Quilted coverlets were usually made of two kinds of fabric, the central field being surrounded by a border of contrasting colour. They were heavily embroidered with gold and silver and were very costly. When the Turkish Bayran bey was ransomed in 1607, he sent a quilted coverlet to the palatine of Hungary with the following letter: "With some difficulty and at great expense, I succeeded in obtaining from the sultan's storehouse this coverlet for you. It is a quilted coverlet worthy of an emperor."

Upholstered chairs were also covered with embroidery, as we know from a letter written by Kata Bethlen: "I have no wooden chairs, for they are all covered with embroidered broad-cloth." In another letter she wrote: "As for the matter concerning the Viennese twistless yarn needed for the chairs, it is not sold by the weight, but in skeins. As for colour, you must choose according to your judgement. My chairs at Sorostély are worked in only four colours: flesh, cerise, green and copper rust. In my opinion, each skein should be of a different colour. The chairs in my house at Kereksora are of six different colours: flesh, green, carmine, sky-blue, orange, and ash-grey. As I have said before, by each colour I understand the colour of each skein, and these are sold at different booths at the market. But you must be careful in your choice. Of each colour, buy several skeins, for once the work has begun, it is difficult to find more of the same." So we learn that chairs were upholstered with broadcloth and stitched with woollen yarn which was sold in skeins.

In Prince Ferenc Rákóczi's castle at Regéc the chairs and benches were decorated with flowers worked in cross-stitch, and with figures in *petit point-gobelin* stitch (Hungarian National Museum). The motifs reflected contemporary European taste.

Coloured woollen yarn was used for the floral patterned chairs, now in the museum, which were embroidered by the women of the Dessewffy family in the middle of the 18th century. The motifs were styled according to contemporary European fashion.

Pomp-loving Hungarians were not content to adorn their tables with the costly creations of the goldsmiths. Tablecloths also had to be ornately embroidered. Often the centre of the cloth showed a wreath enclosing the arms, heraldic animals, and initials of the family. Large tablecloth were stitched with well-proportioned and evenly distributed bouquets and sprays of flowers. Each corner of the border was highlighted by more bouquets and an arcaded trellis of sprigs *(Figs. 42–43)*. When the centre of the cloth was left free of decoration, a densely embroidered and lace-trimmed runner was placed over it. The design matched the pattern of the tablecloth. Whitework, silver and gold, green and dark red silk threads were much favoured. Black-and-white embroidered cloths had black-worked runners when the table was set for a funeral feast. A third category of table-linen was the "border cloth". The entire surface of this long piece of fabric, sixty cm in width, was embroidered. It was hung from the edges of the table, and a tablecloth just large enough to cover the table top was placed over it. In 1672 an inventory was made of goods confiscated from the castle of Vinna. Among these was an item formerly belonging to the wife of István Kecskeméty, which was described as "a cloth picked out in gold, to go around the table". A tablecloth with runner, border, and napkins comprised a complete set of table linen. At large banquets, the servants carried in the dishes on embroidered napkins.

Towels and napkins for drying hands and face were likewise embellished on the narrow ends with gold, silver, coloured and whitework embroidery.

At wedding feasts the witness, the best man, the toast-master, the father of the bride and the chief butler were all provided with napkins specially embroidered for the occasion. In the making of these the wife of Count József Teleki, Kata Bethlen, especially excelled. She and her women embroidered many tablecloths and napkins not only for her own household, but for all her relatives as well. The family correspondence reveals that she was consulted on the choice of patterns and stitches. She knew what was appropriate for each event, and what suited the rank of the chief participants. Before the marriage of Judit Teleki, the daughter of her brother-in-law Sándor Teleki, she wrote: "Concerning the question of the napkins, the witness, the best man and the two toast-masters must have napkins of silver and gold stitch. The host, if he is not a member of the family, must have the same. Silk, gold and silver thread should be used for butlers and cupbearers." She made twenty-three napkins for the wedding, five of which were embroidered in gold and silver, eight in carmine red, and ten in sea-green silk. For variety and brilliance silk threads were mixed with gold and silver from Nuremberg.

Communion cloths are especially noteworthy examples of Hungarian Renaissance embroidery. Eighty to one hundred cm in length, they were made of fine lawn or linen. Many were originally intended for secular use and later donated to the church as pious gifts. Others were betrothal kerchiefs. This is shown by the embroidered inscription on a communion cloth belonging to the Calvinist church of Zsujta in the County of Abaúj. The inscription reads: "On the day of her betrothal Erzsébet Csapó gentlewoman to Esquire Gáspár Pelbarth of Alsó-Vattha June 25, Anno Dni 1718." And: "Donated by Gaspar Pelbarth to the ecclesia of the Helvetian faith of Zuyta [Zsujta]. Novemberis 21, Anno Domini 1721." Some kerchiefs were specifically made for church use. Into these they usually embroidered the donor's name, the date of donation, and the name of the parish. Sometimes long biblical quotations were added in the middle or on the borders. The corners of communion cloths are always the most ornately stitched. The conventional corner design consists of floral forms, bouquets, and undulating vines. The borders of large communion cloths repeat the corner motif, sometimes in a simplified version. In the middle there is sometimes a representation of the *Agnus Dei,* a pelican, or a stag encircled by a wreath. Less often we find the Madonna, Adam and Eve, or the Evangelists, depicted within roundels. On these communion cloths the inscriptions are placed either around the border or inside the wreath.

In the 17th century, Hungarian Renaissance motifs made their appearance on ecclesiastical vestments. On chasubles secular floral motifs were often preferred to representations of saints. Some garments were divided into three embroidered panels, each separated from the other by a narrow band. The middle field was covered with symmetrical floral patterns, the other two with sprays or flowering vines *(Plate VI, Figs. 55, 56)*. Some vestments were covered by a dense pattern of vines and branches interspersed with small animals. Chasubles for poorer churches were made of linen instead of silk or velvet, and the embroidery was also less elaborate. Instead of gold and silver, coloured silk thread was deemed sufficient, and the stitches were larger and less refined. These vestments were usually the work of parishioners who displayed refreshing simplicity and good taste. They covered the divided surfaces with garlands and flowering vines around a centrally placed representation of the Madonna, St. Anne with Two Others *(Mettercia)*, or other saintly figures, thus emphasizing the sacred function of their work. In their simplicity of design and technique, these charming textiles reflect the unpretentious quality of folk art.

Gold and silver embroidery *(skófium)* was either worked with very thin wire, or with metal wires wound around a silk core. For silk embroidery, twistless silk yarns were used. Wool yarn was only rarely employed. Whitework was executed in silk, flax, or cotton.

Among the many stitching techniques the most widely adopted were *satin stitches*. For the filling in of larger surfaces, the needleworker proceeded in straight-across, step, notched, tablet, or zigzag patterns. Long flat stitches were often couched to the foundation in *persian* stitch (laid and couched work). *Counted thread-work* produced patterns which look the same on both sides of the fabric. The characteristic of the so-called *Turkish embroidery* (brick stitch) is that one row of stitches shows up on the face, and the second on the reverse side of the cloth. A typically Hungarian technique, developed in the 17th century is called *point de Hongrie*. This is a shaded embroidery of zigzag patterns worked in multicoloured silk thread. Between each colour or colour groups, rows of gold or silver were introduced. This method could be adopted for the filling in of either large areas or single motifs *(Plate V and Figs. 29, 47)*. *Point de Hongrie* became popular in western and southern Europe during the 17th century. In Genoa, especially, it was used for working the ground of flower-decorated fabrics. While oriental taste showed a preference for the random distribution of colours, *point de Hongrie* introduced refinement into the grouping of colours and thus made decorations more pleasing to Western eyes. Stems and tendrils were worked in chain or stem stitch, or with a loose cross-stitch known in Hungary as *Margaret stitch* (herringbone stitch). The *Italian weaving stitch,* otherwise called *French cross-stitch,* is a kind of counted thread work. Both names are appropriate because the points appear to have been woven on the face, as if worked in cross-stitch on the wrong side of the cloth. Gold and silver embroidery was mostly executed in *couched work* with the metal threads couched with silk.

French knots, or "forget-me-not" dots, created the illusion of rows of pearls when worked in white wool on white. Most white-on-white embroidery was worked in the cutwork or *punto tagliato* technique. On a fine mesh ground some motif areas were left uncut and embroidered with floral designs. Drawn-thread, or *punto tirato* embroidery with geometrical motifs, was frequently used for edging.

The wealth of motifs and colours, as well as the high level of proficiency in technique is a Renaissance development in Hungarian textiles. This art form, however, retained its rich characteristics throughout the centuries.

LACE

The word "lace" immediately conjures up the picture of a delicately wrought, filigree-like textile designed purely for decorative purposes. It was an achievement of the Italian Renaissance. Side by side with the grandiose manifestations of the fine arts, lace contributed grace and airiness to this age.

Between the 11th and 13th centuries Hungarian women were already adorning their heads with gold nets. These were usually put together of knotted strands and *passementerie* (braid). In 1848, when the tomb of Anne de Châtillon (d. 1184), wife of Béla III (1173–1196), was opened in Székesfehérvár, a head-dress was discovered made of crocheted and knotted lace. A similar find, dating from the 14th century, came to light in Bácsmonostor. Other examples come from the crypt of the church in Gyulafehérvár (1907–1918); from the crypt of the Calvinist church in Csenger (1936); and from graves in the cemetery in Boldva. All three locations yielded fragments of knotted gold lace head-dresses sewn together with *passementerie*. All these laces date back to the second half of the 16th century.

Historically, lace falls into two main categories: *needle-point* and *bobbin* lace. Needle-point lace developed directly from cutwork embroidery *(punto tagliato)* in which groups of counted warp and weft threads are removed from the field for decoration by cutting, and the remaining rectangular openings are filled with star motifs. The so-called *reticella* lace, in which the smallest area of the original ground is left, still retains the rectangular openings, and the decorative patterns are of a geometrical design. These patterns, however, became more elaborate during the 16th century. The geometric shapes were gradually replaced by vine leaves, flowers, human and animal figures. The patterns freely flow across the openings and the ground material no longer constitutes an essential part of the decoration.

The Hungarian National Museum owns an outstanding example of so-called *reticella* lace *(Figs. 65–66)*. This piece of lace, made in Venice towards the end of the 16th century, has a ground with square-shaped openings filled with vines, flowers, and figures. The vines issue from a centrally positioned bouquet held by an S-shaped half figure, providing a front view of the body and a profile of the head. The figure is curly-haired and slim-waisted; the dress has a V-shaped neck, and the sleeve is long with a puffed upper section. Beside the figure is an eagle with spread wings. This unique piece of lace was discovered by the author among the discarded costumes of the Academy for Dramatic Art.

As the technique of needle-point lace evolved, lace-makers abandoned the rectangular openings in the foundation thus introducing greater variety and movement into the patterns. This new technique is called *punto in aria,* meaning "stitches in the air". In the middle of the 17th century Venice led the world in the creation of the most exquisite specimens of such Baroque lace.

The development of lace in France was greatly fostered by the two Medici queens, the wives of Henry II and Henry IV, who brought from their country a love and appreciation of lace. Furthermore, in 1664 the French statesman, Jean-Baptiste Colbert began local manufacture, since the importation of lace from Italy and Flanders into France was extremely costly.

Bobbin lace evolved from the art of *macramé* which is the decorative knotting of many single strands of yarn. The initially geometric designs were later replaced by leaf motifs, and still later, adopting the method of plainweave, scroll and floral forms were introduced.

Its most artistic and versatile form is the Baroque bobbin lace which spread from Italy to all parts of Europe in the course of the 16th century.

Bobbin lace developed in Hungary from the manufacture of *passementerie*. It was first produced by the loop-makers and the button-makers who formed their first guild during the reign of King Sigismund. In the 16th century bobbin lace was a domestic craft practised by women commissioned by the loop-makers, their trade being regulated by town edicts. In 1560 it was proclaimed in Selmecbánya that "young unmarried women should be barred from lace-making, for such light and easy work may lead the poorer among them astray. Let them find employment with honest people". It is interesting to note that a similarly worded regulation appeared thirty years later in the Flemish town of Gand. Hungarian craftsmen adopted the technique of ribbon and cut linenwork lace which they enhanced by pomegranate and tulip motifs borrowed from native embroidery patterns. The early popularity of lace in Hungary is evidenced by the large quantities of lace listed in trousseau inventories.

The earliest example of Hungarian-made gold bobbin lace is in the Hungarian National Museum. It was found in 1853 at the opening of the crypt in the Calvinist church of Losonc. Made towards the end of the 16th century, it is one of the earliest examples of bobbin lace or *knotted lace*. It comprises two strips: a scalloped border, and an insert made of square mesh decorated with leaf motifs. The strips are joined and edged with picot which gives unity to the whole. This delicate lace, reminiscent of filigree work, once adorned a woman's dress. It is a fine example of the highly developed art of lace-making in Hungary during the Renaissance.

A similar lace was found in the Avas crypt in Miskolc, but the border and the insert seem to have been used as dress trimmings.

In the 17th century Flanders was famous for her bobbin laces. Brussels, Mechlin and Valenciennes produced many fine varieties and supplied all the neighbouring countries.

Network lace was brought to Europe from the Middle East during the crusades. In this type we may recognize the origins of both needle-point and bobbin lace.

The foundation of network lace is made by knotting together several strands to create a net. The artist then works various embroidery patterns onto this foundation. The technique is different from both needle-point and bobbin lace since two separate methods are employed.

From the 16th century onwards, a variety of lace stitches were developed. Their ingenious selection for the filling in of available spaces produced patterns which liberated the art of lace-making from the earlier stiffness of geometric designs. We can recognize on these laces, too, patterns inspired by the rich floral forms of Hungarian embroidery. Elaborate sheets and altar-cloths are often complemented by wide borders of network lace with pictorial representations of biblical scenes and figures of the saints. These were taken from pattern books which were still in use in the 19th century.

CARPETS

Oriental carpets have always enjoyed great popularity in Europe. In addition to embellishing large halls and small chambers, their brilliance enlivened the sombrely furnished interiors of the past. For many centuries, the Hungarian nobility, gentry, and bourgeoisie considered oriental carpets as an essential accessory to the furnishing of their homes.

As soon as mercantile trade was established between Hungary and Italy in the 14th century, the importation of oriental rugs began through the agency of Venetian merchants. A number of trade centres were established in the northern part of Hungary and in Transylvania. Not only the magnates and prelates, but also the lesser nobility and the merchants of Buda owned many carpets. In 1493 commander Pál Kinizsi recovered many Persian rugs from the Turks who had carried them off earlier as booty. In 1520 Pál Tomori, Archbishop of Kalocsa, put his money and all his valuables into the safekeeping of one Miklós Ládonyi. The inventory included eleven rugs. The will of one Pál Maghy, dated 1529, mentions eight carpets. Four of these were described as old and large, suitable for hanging on the wall; four others were described as "table carpets". In 1539 one Kata Paksy received ten carpets as part of her dowry. In 1564 the estate of Miklós Oláh, Bishop of Esztergom, included one rug, long and red in colour; one table carpet; and a coach with two white rugs. György Szerémy, humanist writer, tells in his memoirs that in the 16th century the walls of rooms were hung with carpets, and the floors were covered with costly rugs "without which no man would set up his tent on a military campaign".

In 1541 a certain István Gyulai owned four large carpets, two others large enough to cover three tables, six more to cover two tables, and seven small rugs. In 1571 an inventory was made of the possessions of György Thury. It listed thirty-nine carpets. In 1579 a certain Mátyás Zaberdini Horvát and his sister divided their inheritance. Horvát received four medium size white, and three red carpets. His sister's share was one medium size white, one large and three small red rugs. Anna Máriássy's will dated 1592 mentions one white rug dotted with black. The poet János Rimay, who was major-domo in the household of István Bocskay, and Gábor Bethlen, princes of Transylvania, was sent on missions to Turkey in 1608, 1620 and 1621. Accounts of his purchases list one carpet sprinkled with white, and three others with bird designs, all to be used as table coverings. In 1622 Gábor Bethlen sent one Pál Keresztesi to Constantinople where he bought six Turkish scarlet rugs, eleven blue divan Persian rugs, two old silk, and eight smaller silk carpets.

Carpets were frequently bequeathed to the Church. In 1525 noblewoman Dorottya Kanizsay left three to the chapel of Bajcs, and four for the adornment of the chapel of St. Ladislas in Valpó. In 1557 Pál Bornemissza, Bishop of Nyitra and Transylvania, bequeathed several carpets "for the embellishment of the Church of Nyitra". In 1646, the nobleman István Bethlen bequeathed to a church three white Persian, five silk, and three red Persian rugs. He also left two red Persian rugs to László Rédey which, in his own words "used to cover my seat in church, and of which he should make use likewise".

In 1648 István Csatóházi Móré made a bequest of carpets to the Jesuit and Franciscan fathers of the church in Szendrő.

Inventories inform us about the type, size, and use of carpets. They also give evidence of carpets in the homes of the well-to-do burghers. In the will drawn up by Sebestyén Beis of Nagyszombat in 1605, there is a reference to "a long trestle table covered with a red carpet", and one white rug. In 1610 Tamás, Sándor, and Ilona Viczay received a legacy including twenty rugs from one Zsuzsanna Maróthy. Among them were table carpets, red, white, Persian and Turkish rugs, and a white Persian carpet with bird motifs. When Ilona Thurzó married aristocrat Gáspár Illésházy in 1614, she was given two red rugs for her coach, while her husband received two old white Turkish, and three red carpets, as well as a green table carpet. There are two paintings of this couple laid out in state, one dating from 1648, the other from 1655. Both are in the National Museum, and in both, the bier is covered with Turkish rugs.

In 1650 a certain Krisztina Tassy received, as part of her marriage portion, two small oriental table carpets. According to the 1669 inventory of the Castle of Ecsed, there were several rugs in each room in the castle. Of the one hundred and twenty carpets, thirty were used as wall-hangings. Rugs also feature in a description of the treasury of Count Ferenc Nádasdy (1670): "There are eight Turkish silk rugs woven of gold and silver thread, two of which are sufficiently long to cover the cupboard one and a half times."

In 1671 an inventory was taken of the confiscated treasures of Count István Thököly's castle at Árva. This inventory provides us with the names by which oriental carpets were designated in Hungary. Rugs made in Persia were called *"tapetes persici, vulgo 'divan' carpets"*, while rugs originating from Asia Minor were referred to as *"tapetes turcici, vulgo 'scarlet' carpets"*. (Then, as now, carpets were designated according to their place of manufacture.)

Carpets from Asia Minor basically fall into two groups depending on their decorative style. In the first category are rugs with stylized geometric designs: *Holbein* rugs, *Ushaks* ornamented with arabesques, white *Ushaks, bird* and *pellet* rugs. Carpets belonging to the second category are richly adorned with stylized floral designs: the *Ghiordes, Ladik* and *Kula* prayer rugs, and the *small* and *large Ushaks*. One kind of *Kula* is the mourning rug or *cemetery Kula*. Another type of rug is known as *Transylvanian,* so named because most of them have been found in Transylvania.

The sumptuous ornamentation and the wide range of colours characterizing the Transylvanian carpets reflect the Persian influence on the art of weaving, which reached its zenith in the 16th and 17th centuries. Persian carpet-making also had an influence on Turkish weavers.

The merchants of Transylvania kept up a brisk exchange of goods with the Orient. They imported a large number of carpets, many of which were eventually donated to churches. In 1933 ninety-eight arabesque *Ushaks* were counted in the Lutheran churches of Transylvania. The so-called Black Cathedral of Brassó was furnished with one hundred and nineteen oriental rugs. Hungarian weavers, influenced by carpets imported from Asia Minor, also produced knotted rugs. Of these there is only one surviving example, now in the Hungarian National Museum. The stars and geometric medallions in the border design are typical Transylvanian motifs. The field, which is of a deep blue colour, features the conventionalized floral patterns of Hungarian Renaissance embroidery. The upper end of the field bears the letters D. S. and the date 1723 *(Fig. 79)*.

Although the National Museum collection is not extensive, every piece is nevertheless an outstanding example of the art of rug weaving in Asia Minor; furthermore, all the different types are represented in the collection.

*

The aim of this book is to acquaint the reader with the manifold aspects of the rich collection of textiles in the Hungarian National Museum. A complete survey has not been possible, for the collection includes more than ten thousand pieces. Such an extensive collection, however, does provide valuable insight into the festive and every-day occasions of life in Hungary's past, some of which, it is hoped, has reached the reader through these pages.

BIBLIOGRAPHY

Medieval and Renaissance Textiles

	Legendae Sancti Regis Stephani. Hungarian translation and annotation by ELEMÉR VARJÚ. Budapest, 1928.
KOVÁCS, É.:	"Casula Sancti Stephani Regis." *Acta Historiae Artium* V (1958), fasc. 3–4. pp. 181–222.
POGÁNY, K.:	"A sztropkói miseruha" [The Sztropkó Chasuble]. *Archaeologiai Értesítő,* (1907), pp. 411–431.
KEMÉNY, L.:	"Hol készült a sztropkói casula?" [The Origin of the Sztropkó Chasuble]. *Archaeologiai Értesítő,* (1909), pp. 218–221.
	Régi egyházművészet országos kiállítása [National Exhibition of Ancient Eccleciastical Art, catalogue by K. CsÁNYI]. Budapest, 1930.
CSERNYÁNSZKY, M.:	*Az Esztergomi főszékesegyház paramentumai* [Paraments of the Esztergom Cathedral]. Budapest, 1933.
GEREVICH, T.:	*Magyarország románkori emlékei* [Hungarian Romanesque Antiquities]. Budapest, 1938.
BALOGH, J.:	"Botticelli-Zeichnungen für Stickereien." *Acta Historiae Artium* V (1959), pp. 298–308.
BÁRÁNYNÉ, OBERSCHALL, M.:	*Magyarországi miseruhák* [Hungarian Chasubles]. Budapest, 1937.
SCHUETTE, M.–MÜLLER CHRISTENSEN, S.:	*Das Stickereiwerk.* Tübingen, 1963. Ill. 23–26.

Hand-woven Textiles

MIHALIK, GY.–TÖRÖK, K.:	"Szövött munkák" [Woven Fabrics]. In: *Iparművészet könyve* [Book of Applied Arts]. Ed. by GYÖRGY RÁTH. Budapest, 1912, pp. 461–576.
BOBROVSZKY, I.:	*Spätmittelalterliche Leinentücher.* Budapest, 1970.

The Dossal of King Matthias's Throne

	"Hunyadi címeres pluviale Boszniában" [Pluvial with the Hunyadi Crest in Bosnia]. *Archaeologiai Értesítő,* (1874), p. 104.
	"A király legfelsőbb elhatározása" [Proclamation of His Royal Highness]. In: *Budapesti Közlöny,* (1886), p. 203.
LUBÓCZY, ZS.	"Első Mátyás király trónszőnyegei" [The Throne Dossals of King Matthias I]. *Archaeologiai Értesítő,* (1887), pp. 404–417.
CZOBOR, B.:	"Erdődi Bakócz Tamás kárpitja" [A Hanging from the Bakócz Legacy]. *Archaeologiai Értesítő,* (1889), pp. 120–131, 203–217.
FRAKNÓI, V.:	"Erdődi Bakócz Tamás műtárgyai" [Art Treasures

	of Tamás Erdődi Bakócz]. *Archaeologiai Értesítő*, (1889), pp. 120–131, 20:–217.
Radisics, J.:	"Mátyás király trónkárpitja" [The Throne Dossal of King Matthias]. *Magyar Iparművészet* XIV. (1911), Ill. 354–357.
Falke, O. v.:	*Kunstgeschichte der Seidenweberei*. Berlin, 1913, pp. 114, 546.
Santangelo, A.:	*Tessuti d'arti italiane*. Milano, 1959.
Balogh, J.:	*A művészet Mátyás király udvarában. I–II* [Art in the Court of King Matthias. I–II]. Budapest, 1966. I: p. 392, II: Ill. 627, 630.
Balogh, J.:	"L'arte italiana in Ungheria." *La Vie d'Italia* XXXVI, (1930), pp. 665–666.

Belt of Vladislav II's Papal Sword

Fingerlin, I.:	*Gürtel des hohen und späten Mittelalters*. München, 1971.
Kalmár, J.:	"II. Ulászló pápai díszkardja 1509-ből" [Vladislav II's Papal Sword from 1509]. *Magyar Nemzeti Múzeum Történeti Műkincsei*. Budapest, no date.

Hungarian Embroidery in the 16th and 17th Centuries

Csernyánszky, M.:	*Magyar úrihímzésű miseruhák* [Embroidered Chasubles from the Hungarian Renaissance]. Budapest, 1942.
Palotay, G.:	*Oszmán-török elemek a magyar hímzésben* [Ottoman Turkish Motifs in Hungarian Embroidery]. Budapest, 1940.
Balogh, J.:	*Az erdélyi renaissance* [The Renaissance in Transylvania]. Kolozsvár, 1943. Ill. 275, 276.
Varjú-Ember, M.:	*Alte ungarische Stickerei*. Budapest, 1963.
Balogh, J.:	*A népművészet és a történeti stílusok* [The Folk Art and the Historical Styles]. Budapest, 1967.
V. Ember, M.:	"A textilgyűjtemény új hímzései" [New Acquisitions: Embroidery]. *Folia Archaeologica*, (1971), pp. 219–235.
V. Ember, M.:	"A XVII. századi magyar hímzések motívumkincse" [Decorative Motifs in 17th Century Hungarian Embroidery]. *Folia Historiae*, (1972), pp. 45–80.
Kendrick, A. F.:	*English Domestic Embroidery*. London, 1904.

Laces

Csernyánszky, M.:	*Ungarische Spitzenkunst*. Budapest, 1962.
V. Ember, M.:	*A csipke* [Lace]. Budapest, 1961.
V. Ember, M.:	"Reneszánsz csipkék" [Renaissance Lace]. *Folia Archaeologica*, (1955), pp. 175–181.

Carpets

CSERNYÁNSZKY, M.:	*Erdélyi szőnyegek* [Rugs from Transylvania]. Budapes,t 1944.
CSERNYÁNSZKY, M.:	*Az Iparművészeti Múzeum török szőnyegei* [Turkish Rugs in the Museum of Applied Arts]. Budapest, 1946.
BATÁRI, F.:	*Alte anatolische Teppiche.* Graz, 1974.
GOMBOS, K.:	*Régi keleti szőnyegek* [Oriental Rugs from the Past]. Christian Museum, Esztergom, 1977.

LIST OF PLATES AND FIGURES

I, 1–2 CHASUBLE

Red velvet brocade with embroidered pillar orphrey.

The pattern shows doves crowned by golden aureoles set among white stars. No similar decorative motifs have been found on Italian-made textiles, but the technique is closely related to Venetian brocades of the same period. The fabric was probably woven in Venice c. 1400. The ground of the orphrey is worked in laid spun gold, couched with silk thread and patterned with rayed suns. The style is typical of south German, Silesian, Polish, Moravian and Hungarian embroidery of the period. The figures and the architectural details are made with the subtly shaded stitches characteristic of needle painting. St. John, St. Margaret, and Mary on the front of the chasuble were the work of one workshop and show strong Italian influence. The figure of St. Elizabeth was appliquéd several decades later over the upper part of the orphrey.

c. 1400.

Length: 108 cm. Width: 78 cm. Cat. No.: 1953.147.

3 CHASUBLE

Green velvet ground with a scatter design of red and white flowers.

The ground of the cross-orphrey has a pattern of rosettes, and the embroidery is worked by the needle-painting method. The figure of Christ is shown on the Mount of Olives surrounded by the sleeping apostles Peter, James, and John. Below, framed by pillars, Christ is bound to a pillar. In the bottom section the half-figure of the Redeemer, wearing a crown of thorns, can be seen. The velvet is of Venetian manufacture, dating from the beginning of the 15th century. The embroidery is of South German–Northern Hungarian provenance.

c. 1400.

Length: 101 cm. Width: 74 cm. Cat. No.: 1953.145.

4 CHASUBLE

Velvet brocade interwoven with gold thread on atlas ground.

The design is asymmetrical, composed of entwined leafy branches. The branches and stylized leaves are woven in gold thread. The spaces between the branches are filled in with sprays of vine. The pillar, of the cross-shaped orphrey is divided into three fields. The upper section shows the enthroned St. Anne with Jesus and Mary on a raised ground of geometric stitchery. The middle section bears the crowned figure of St. Catherine under a square, crenellated arch. She holds a sword in her right hand, and a wheel in her left, symbols of her martyrdom. Below, framed by a similar arch, appears the figure of St. Margaret with the dragon. When the chasuble was altered, the lower part of this field was cut off. A kneeling angel is placed on each arm of the cross-orphrey. The figures are embroidered in needle painting. The folds of the angels' robes are embellished with gold stars.

The chasuble was purchased by the museum from the bishopric of Szepes.

The brocade was woven in Venice in the second half of the 15th century.

The needlework is of north Hungarian origin, dating from the second quarter of the 15th century.
Length: 100 cm. Width: 72 cm. Cat. No.: 1917.42.4.

5 ORPHREY

Coloured silk embroidered with gold and silver.

The slender figure of Christ is shown on a cross entwined with green branches. Above him sits King David. On the arms of the cross-orphrey we see the half-figures of two prophets. The figure of Mary Magdalene at the foot of the crucified Christ was mutilated when the chasuble was recut for alteration.

Hungarian, mid-15th century.
Length: 103 cm. Width: 59 cm. Cat. No.: 1953.164.

6 CHASUBLE

Blue *ferronerie* velvet brocade with embroidered cross-orphrey.

The velvet is partly voided, partly woven with gold thread, with vine and pomegranate motifs. The orphrey has a couched gold ground of laid-work embroidery. It is almost entirely filled with a needle-painted, fork-shaped, and leafy cross *(arbor vitae)* surmounted by the slender figure of Christ. The figures of Mary, John, and Mary Magdalene are at the foot of the cross. The arms of the orphrey bear the half-figures of prophets, and mottos. The section above Christ's head with its half-figure and the lower section were partially cut away when the chasuble was altered. The cold colour-scheme, the two-dimensional figural representation, and the heavy fall of drapery on this Hungarian embroidery are rather striking. The *arbor vitae* is a motif rarely encountered in embroidery.

The brocade was manufactured in Venice in the first half of the 15th century. The embroidery is Hungarian workmanship dating from the middle of the 15th century.
Length: 103 cm. Width: 75 cm. Cat. No.: 1953.143.

7–8 PLUVIAL

Faded blue velvet with embroidery in silver thread.

The fabric has pattern of wheat sheaves in a radial arrangement. The lower part bears the monogram AEIOV, and the date 1448. The shield shows the Annunciation on a rosette-sprinkled field. The figures are worked in needle painting. Mary's robe has a wheat grain motif. Around the two figures appears the motto: *Ave Maria gratia, Ecce ancilla Domini, fiat mihi secundum verbum tuum.*

The pluvial was discovered by art historian Flóris Rómer in 1864, in the sacristy of the church in Tököl.

German workmanship from the first half of the 15th century.
Length: 148 cm. Width: 283 cm. Shield: 39×44 cm. Cat. No.: 1953.128.

9 CHASUBLE

Gold brocade shot with silver.

The ground is red silk patterned with cornucopias filled with pomegranates and surrounded by vine wreaths. On the back the figure of the Madonna, holding the Infant Jesus, is in the centre of a glory of sunrays. Two small angels hold a crown over her head. Above, St. Anne is seen seated with the infants Jesus and Mary in a quatrefoil. Two more quatrefoils enclose St. Andrew and St. John on each side of the Madonna. The pedimental figure of James the Apostle is seen below. The front of the chasuble is decorated with the highly plastic half-figures of John, James and Andrew. The richly drawn folds of their robes are worked in *or nué*.

The chasuble was purchased by the museum from the Roman Catholic church of Kőszeg. The brocade is of Florentine manufacture, probably made around 1470 in the workshop of Malocchi. The embroidery is Austrian–South German work, early 16th century.

Length: 115 cm. Width: 78 cm. Cat. No.: 1908.70.

10 CHASUBLE

Red velvet brocade with cross-orphrey in relief embroidery.

The pomegranate pattern is raised on a gold ground. The orphrey is the work of Hungarian needle-craftsmen. The Madonna with Child stands under an ogee arch supported by pillars. Below the figure of Mary appear St. Barbara and probably St. Dorothy, whose left hand with her insignia is missing. The two arms of the cross show angels kneeling in adoration. The faces and hands are embroidered in needle painting, the robes are worked in *or nué* technique. The architectural motifs, the proportional arrangement of the decorative elements, the stance of the figures and the folds of the robes are characteristic of the Gothic style. The drawing and execution of patterns show the mixture of Italian and German influence typical of 15th and 16th century Hungarian art.

The brocade is in the Venetian style from the latter part of the 15th century. The embroidery was made in Hungary towards the end of the 15th century.

Length: 121 cm. Width: 77 cm. Cat. No.: 1954.661.

II, 11–12 CHASUBLE

Wine-red silk velvet with cross-orphrey embroidered in silk and gold worked in needle-painting technique.

The ground of the orphrey is couched gold embroidery. The upper part shows the Last Judgement with Christ sitting on a rayed throne. On his right is the kneeling figure of Mary. Below her the gates of Heaven can be seen with Gothic arches, and the small unclothed figures of the Redeemed. On Christ's left kneels John the Baptist. Behind him are the damned with the devil, and the open jaws of a dragon, symbolizing the gates of Hell. The representation of the Crucifixion is most artfully executed. The slender body of the crucified Christ rises above a group of five figures. The fainting Mary is supported on one side, while on the other stands the apostle John. Behind them the praying figures of a man and a woman are visible. The graceful curve of this group of figures completes the picture. The Annunciation is represented on the lower part of the orphrey. This was originally on the front of the chasuble, and consequently does not fit in with the rest of the thematic features of the decoration. The composition, however, is quite perfect. By a skilful use of the available surface the Angel is made to appear behind the kneeling Mary, a typically Flemish styling. The anatomical details of the embroidered figures reveal superb craftsmanship. The masterly use of needle painting brings alive the facial expressions, and the shapes of the bodies under the folds of the robes are successfully suggested.

In the 1474 inventory of the town of Kassa there is a reference to a chasuble made in the workshop of a local artist for the church of Sztropkó. The embroidery, based on a cartoon designed in the Netherlands, was made by a Hungarian craftsman who succeeded in recreating, even in the colour-scheme, the beauty of the original drawing.

The museum purchased the chasuble from the church of Sztropkó through the mediation of Bishop Ágost Fischer-Colbrie of Kassa.

Late 15th century.

Length: 104 cm. Width: 76 cm. Cat. No.: 1908.70.

13–14 CHASUBLE

Red velvet with plain and loop-woven brocade.

The pattern shows large pineapples, thistles, and leaves. The orphrey is embroidered in raised gold thread and depicts the figures of John the Baptist and the martyrs St. Lawrence and St. Stephen, under Romanesque arches. On the arms of the cross are the half-figures of St. Helen and St. Lucy. The faces and hands are worked in needle painting, the clothing in *or nué* technique. The brocade was manufactured in Venice in the second half of the 15th century. The needlework is Florentine dating from between 1470 and 1480.

Length: 101 cm. Width: 74 cm. Cat. No.: 1953.150.

15 CHASUBLE

Red velvet brocade with pomegranate and leaf motifs partly woven into the foundation with gold thread, partly "carved out" of the velvet.

The ground of the orphrey is worked in raised gold embroidery. The vertical section shows three saints—Peter, Paul and James—under domed arches. The faces and hands are done in needle painting, the clothing in *or nué* technique. The horizontal section depicts the Annunciation.

The brocade was woven in Venice in the last quarter of the 15th century. The embroidery, also Venetian, was probably made around 1470.

Length: 103 cm. Width: 73 cm. Cat. No.: 1953.153.

16 CHASUBLE

Red and green velvet brocade shot with gold.

The pattern consists of pomegranates within vine tracery tied with crowns. The pillar of the orphrey has a design of alternating cartouches and round medallions in couched embroidery. The upper part shows Christ Resurrected; the middle and lower sections depict St. Michael and St. John the Evangelist, respectively. On the arms of the cross the Annunciation is enclosed in semicircular arcs. The figures are worked in finely stitched needle painting. The embroidery is Italian as evidenced by the remarkable resemblance of Mary and the angel to two paintings of the Annunciation by Botticelli (Uffizi Gallery, Florence, Art Gallery, Glasgow).

The chasuble was a gift to the museum from the Hungarian government.

The brocade is of a Venetian type. The embroidery is Italian. Both *c*. 1500.

Length: 97 cm. Width: 72 cm. Cat. No.: 1929.50.

17 CHASUBLE

Gold brocade patterned with flowers in garlands of leaves.

The cross-orphrey has a leaf design on a raised gold ground. The medallions show biblical scenes executed in *or nué* technique : the Flight from Egypt, the Presentation of Jesus in the Temple, the Birth of Jesus, while the Assumption replaces what chronologically should have been the Visitation. The scene of the Assumption is mutilated, showing only the head of Mary. The rest was cut away when the garment was altered. On the arms of the cross we see the Annunciation. Between the medallions are the symbols of the Evangelists John, Mark and Luke.

The brocade is of Florentine provenance from the second half of the 15th century.

The embroidery was made in Italy after a drawing by either Botticelli or Filippino Lippi in the early part of the 16th century.

Length: 108 cm. Width: 77 cm. Cat. No.: 1953.139.

18 HANDWOVEN CLOTH

Linen, interwoven with blue cotton threads.

The middle of the cloth has a wide band patterned with towered bastions and human figures. On either side narrow strips show birds, stars, letters, and rosettes. Donated by the Roman Catholic church of Bártfa.

Hungarian work from the second half of the 15th century.

Length: 105 cm. Width: 65 cm. Cat. No.: 1915.3.

19 PILLOW

Linen pillow-slip interwoven with blue cotton threads.

On one side the slip shows the Fountain of Life between two oxen and against a leafy tree within a wide band. On either side a narrow band has stylized letter motifs. On the other side of the slip the design of the wide band is repeated with additional features showing a spring and two birds resembling turkeys between trees.

Donated by Kornél Divald.

Hungarian, from the first half of the 16th century.

Length: 43 cm. Width: 42 cm. Cat. No.: 1916.48.

20 THE DOSSAL OF KING MATTHIAS'S THRONE

Gold brocade with green velvet contours.

The foundation is woven of yellow and green silk. A second brocading weft of gold covers the entire surface worked in plain weave in the ground and in looped pile within the design. The wide border shows wings, cornucopias and ears of wheat. The decoration of the field is divided into three areas: the upper third has pomegranates issuing from cornucopias; below, the quartered shield of King Matthias is enclosed in a wreath of oak-leaves and fruits; the lower third section is occupied by a large and ornate dish on tiles. On each side of the vessel stands an eagle poised for flight. Above their heads the cascading ribbons of the wreath terminate in tasselled ends.

The dossal was woven in the Florentine workshop of Francesco Malocchi. The pattern was designed by Pollaiuolo. After the king's death, the dossal became the possession of Archbishop Tamás Bakócz. Later it passed into the hands of a Transylvanian family who eventually donated it to the Hungarian National Museum.

Florence, *c.* 1470. Length: 252 cm. Width: 162 cm. Cat. No.: 1960.190

21 CEREMONIAL SWORD BELT

Gold brocade with outlines woven in red.

A repeating design including the oak-tree of the Rovere arms, the papal tiara with crossed keys, and vines with oak-leaves and acorns. The ends terminate in silver-gilt buckles embellished with blue enamel. The openings of the fifteen pairs of buckle-tongues are also of silver-gilt. In 1932, when the treasures of the former Austro-Hungarian Empire were divided between the two countries, the belt was given to the National Museum.

It is the work of the Italian master-weaver Bernardo Ser Silvano, dated 1509.

Length: 227 cm. Width: 5.7 cm. Cat. No.: 55.3235.

22 PILLOW-SLIP

Fine white linen, decorated at one narrow end with red silk and gold and silver thread.

The width of the embroidered end is 23 cm. The wide middle band has an undulating vine design with large, five-petalled tulips, and sprays of flowers and leaves. Rosettes occupy the spaces between the tulips. The two narrow borders show two kinds of pomegranates strung on a vine. The continuous pattern of undulating vines and flowers is typical of both Italian and Hungarian Renaissance decoration.

The stitches are worked in figured satin stitch. Each of the three different coloured threads is used for separate motifs within the design.

Transylvania, mid-17th century.

Length: 90 cm. Width: 70 cm. Cat. No.: 1954.642.

23 EMBROIDERED END OF A PILLOW-SLIP

Fine white lawn embroidered with red silk and gold threads.

The design of the wide middle band is composed of flower bouquets, alternately in reverse direction, and joined together by S-shaped vines. The central branches bear pomegranates with serrated inner edges. Each fruit is topped by a tulip. The secondary branches have pears, berries and leaves. Between each group is a bow, looped in a figure of eight, and dotted with French knots. From the bows issue pomegranate blossoms in an upward and downward curve. In the narrow borders small pomegranates and five-petalled tulips alternate on a long vine with tendrils. The silk threads are worked in slanting satin stitches, the gold threads in flat, geometrically couched, satin stitches.

Formerly owned by the Wolfner family.

Made in Northern Hungary, mid-17th century.

Length: 62 cm. Width: 17 cm. Cat. No.: 1955.420.

24 PILLOW-SLIP

White silk taffeta, with coloured silk, gold and silver embroidery.

The wide middle band has a repeating pattern of pomegranates, tulips, and stylized carnations. On the scrolling vines birds stand back to back, each holding a flower in its beak. In the two narrow bands carnations with four-leaved stems alternate with single flowers. The pomegranates and the tulips are realistic, while the carnations were made in an exuberant Baroque style. Shaded satin stitches in silk and couched gold and silver laidwork alternate in patches of colour.

Formerly in the collection of the Wolfner family.
Transylvania, second half of the 17th century.
Length: 218 cm. Width: 70 cm. Cat. No.: 1955.447.

25 EMBROIDERED END OF A PILLOW-SLIP
Fine linen with red silk and gold embroidery.
The chief motif of the wide middle band consists of a repeating pattern of two S-shaped garlands sprouting floral branches and leaves. The two garlands are joined together by a ring which also encircles a large pomegranate. The sectional design and the ring of dots relieve the otherwise rigid drawing of the fruit. The triplet of flowers and the five-petalled tulips show a tendency towards Baroque exuberance. The severity of the symmetrical composition is alleviated by the alternate use of red and gold threads. The two narrow bands have a repeating design of small pomegranates and tulips.
The patterns are worked in slanted and chevron satin stitch.
Formerly in the collection of the Wolfner family.
Transylvania, third quarter of the 17th century.
Length: 87 cm. Width: 20 cm. Cat. No.: 1955.438.

26 EMBROIDERED END OF A PILLOW-SLIP
Thin white linen with cutwork embroidery in yellowed white silk thread.
The wide inner strip shows pomegranates. Each fruit is encircled by two large lobed leaves of ornate design. On either side of this broad band three narrow strips have an alternating pattern of tulips, pomegranates and leaves. Every second opening of the square mesh ground is overcast with a cross-stitch. The pattern, identical on both right and reverse sides, is geometrically stitched laidwork.
Formerly in the Wolfner collection.
Northern Hungary, second half of the 17th century.
Length: 70 cm. Width: 45 cm. Cat. No.: 1955.502.

27 PILLOW-SLIP
Thin white linen embroidered with red, blue, green, pink, yellow and brown silk, and gold silver thread.
The embroidered decoration borders three sides of the slip. Two corners have large five-petalled tulips stemming from springs of leaves. From the base of each flower scrolling vines issue to the left and right, terminating in a cinqfoil. The bird standing on the vine is a raven. A carnation occupies the centre of the narrow end with two stylized floral forms on either side. The three flower stems are embraced by a ring from which two vines with tendrils, acanthus blossoms, and large leaves run toward the corners. On the two long sides the carnation motif and a simpler version of the corner motif are repeated. The fine geometric stitchery and the subtle variation of coloured, gold and silver surfaces produce a very pleasing overall effect. The embroidery on both sides of the fabric is identical, worked in tiny satin stitches. The stems, vines, and some of the flower contours are done in slanting satin stitch.
Transylvania, mid-17th century.
Length: 84 cm. Width: 75 cm. Cat. No.: 1955.456.

IV, 28 PILLOW-SLIP

Fine lawn, with embroidery in coloured silk and gold thread.

Three sides are decorated with free-standing motifs. Each corner has an intricately drawn flower. A simpler variation of the same is repeated at the end of the sides and half way along each side is a pineapple on a bed of leaves. The centre of the fruit is further embellished by a lily. Tiny peonies and leaves growing from each side of the fruit give this pattern a dainty appearance.

The motifs and the border design of scrolling vines reflect the style of the Renaissance. The needlework, done in very small slanting satin stitch, is identical on both sides of the fabric and emphasizes the outlines of the motifs. The edging is gold bobbin lace dating from the beginning of the 18th century.

Purchased by the museum from Dr. Károly Csányi.

Hungarian, c. 1650.

Length: 82 cm. Width: 68 cm. Cat. No.: T.1970.1.

V, 29 SHEET

Thin white linen embroidered with red, pink, light and medium blue, green, yellow and mustard silk, and gold and silver thread.

The chief motif consists of two alternating groups of three-stemmed floral sprays. One group shows an acanthus blossom and a tulip in full bloom, the other a tulip, pomegranate and clustered flowerets. The two groups are linked together by a curling vine bearing a rose and a corn-flower. The base of the flowers rests on stylized leaves. The two narrow ends of the sheet are also embroidered. When used as a quilted coverlet, these ends would be folded back to show off the beauty of the embroidery. The stylized motifs are typical of Renaissance decoration. The intricate distribution of coloured, gold and silver surfaces creates shadowy effects. The technique is *point de Hongrie*. The stems, vines and tendrils are worked in slanting stem stitch.

Formerly in the Wolfner collection.

Transylvania, mid-17th century.

Length: 262 cm. Width: 204 cm. Dimensions of embroidery: 180×36 cm. Cat. No.: 1955.458.

30 PILLOW-FACE

Whitework embroidery on thin white linen.

The design consists of three-petalled tulips, pomegranates enclosed in serrated leaves crowned by a tulip, and vines curling around the fruits and flowers. The vine segments begin below the pomegranate in the middle of each side and end at the base of the tulips situated in each corner. The corners are further embellished by an elaborate bouquet of leaves. The centres of the tulips and pomegranates are worked in filet-embroidery, similar to lace. The flowers, vines and decorative dots are stitched in French knots. The outlines, tendrils and small leaves are worked in stem stitch. The main line of motifs runs between two rows of scalloped French knots.

Formerly in the collection of the Wolfner family.

Northern Hungary, mid-17th century.

Length: 75 cm. Width: 75 cm. Cat. No.: 1955.514.

31 DETAIL OF EMBROIDERED SHEET BORDER

Fine linen with embroidery in light-green silk and silver thread.

The design is centred around a pomegranate with sickle-shaped leaves. Attached to it by a double ring and curling away to left and right, S-shaped vines bear tulips and pomegranates. The composition reflects the style of the Renaissance. The distribution of green and silver threads and the conventionalized character of the large leaves show Persian influence. The stitches are identical on the right and reverse sides of the fabric. The technique is satin stitch.

Formerly in the Wolfner collection.

Transylvania, mid-17th century.

Length: 70 cm. Width: 31 cm. Cat. No.: 1955.407.

32 SHEET BORDER

Thin white linen embroidered with red, blue and cream silk, gold and silver thread.

On three sides the narrow outer border shows pomegranates between serrated leaves. The field has floral motifs pointing in opposite directions. The quadrangular disposition of each floral group is typical of Renaissance decoration. The bouquets are composed of stylized carnations, leaves, naturalistically drawn pomegranates, tulips, and pears. The rhythmic sequence of colouring shows oriental influence. The motifs are worked in small slanting satin stitch and geometrically couched flat stitch.

Formerly in the collection of the Wolfner family.

Northern Hungary, third quarter of the 17th century.

Length: 143 cm. Width: 43.5 cm. Cat. No.: 1955.422.

33 SHEET BORDER

Loosely woven cream-coloured linen, embroidered in coloured silk and silver thread.

The pattern consists of flower stems and pomegranates pointing in opposite directions above and below a vine-scroll motif. The colouring of the leaves produces a shaded effect. Small rosettes break up the curving vines. Above and below each rosette a spray of pomegranate blossom issues from the petals. The composition is Renaissance in style. The distribution of colours, and the conventionalized patterns point to Turco-Persian influence. The stitching is identical on both sides of the cloth. The motifs are worked over counted threads of the fabric. The slanting, closely spaced and short stitches evenly cover the surface of each motif. The silver threads are worked in satin stitch.

Formerly in the Wolfner collection.

Hungarian, mid-17th century.

Length: 153 cm. Width: 46 cm. Cat. No.: 1955.423.

34–35 SHEET BORDER

Thin white linen with cutwork *(punto tagliato)* embroidery in yellowed white silk.

Every second opening of the square mesh ground is overcast with cross stitch. The patterns are wrought on the uncut linen foundation, and their outlines follow a zigzag line. The design consists of two kinds of three-stemmed floral sprays issuing from a common stem and separated by the undulating curve of a leaf-vine. Pomegranates spread their branches from this vine toward the flowers. Along the uneven edges a secondary outline of diagonal stitches and picot brings out the beauty of the individual floral motifs, and tones down the rigidity of the design. The technique is geometrical satin stitch.

The stylistic conception is typically Renaissance, similar to the embroidered border of sheet No. 1955.423 (Fig. 33).

Northern Hungary, third quarter of the 17th century.

Length: 190 cm. Width: 41.5 cm. Cat. No.: 1955.504.

36 SHEET BORDER

White-on-white linen embroidery.

The pattern shows a row of large pomegranates with lobed leaves, and rosettes sprouting from between the lobes. An S-shaped festoon of leaves and small pomegranates interlace the chief elements of the design. The embroidery, identical on the right and reverse sides of the fabric, is worked in satin stitch. The stems, garlands and outlines are done in stem stitch. The centre of the fruits and some of the leaves are cutwork embroidery. The edging of 18 cm wide bobbin lace shows a serpentine ribbon pattern.

Formerly in the collection of the Wolfner family.

Northern Hungary, end of the 17th century.

Length: 173 cm. Width: 46.5 cm. Cat. No.: 1955.508.

37 SHEET BORDER

Thin white linen with cutwork and white silk, satin stitch embroidery.

The ground of the cutwork is an extremely fine square mesh, resembling loose weave. The undulating leaf garland bears fully opened roses and carnations. The lower border is edged with 11 cm wide Hungarian bobbin lace showing an intricately drawn ribbon motif. The garland is done in satin stitch, the petals either in satin stitch or filet darning. The middle of the roses is reticella type needle-point lace. The pattern is similar to that of pillow-slip No. 1960.132 in the museum's collection, but is modified according to the requirements of network technique.

Formerly in the Wolfner collection.

Northern Hungary, third quarter of the 17th century.

Length: 170 cm. Width: 50 cm. Cat. No.: 1955.501.

38 SHEET BORDER

Very fine cambric with gold and silver embroidery.

The design of the wide middle band shows a row of tulip-crowned pomegranates and five-petalled tulips. Each motif is enclosed in a garland of serrated and lobed leaves. The garlands are laced together by bows. Small tulips issue from the leaves of the garland. On each side is an outer band of closed and open pomegranates linked by a conventional vine motif. The technique is couched work in fine white silk thread worked in a geometrical pattern. The couching varies with each motif, which is alternately worked in gold and silver threads. The design is a more recent version of a similarly embroidered pillow-slip end Cat. No. 1955.400, (Fig. 39) worked in dark red and gold and dating from the middle of the 17th century.

This piece was purchased by the museum from the collection of Dr. Károly Csányi.

Hungarian, early 18th century.

Length: 89 cm. Width: 24 cm. Cat. No.: T.1970.2.

39 Embroidered end of a pillow-slip

White linen, embroidered with dark red silk and gold threads.

The wider middle band has an alternating pattern of rosettes with spurs. The rosettes are encircled by four serrated leaves. There is a tulip in the triangular space between the leaves. The two narrow bands have a continuous pattern of flower sprigs with three stems. The arrangement of the motifs is typically Renaissance, featuring patterns symmetrically deployed above and below an imaginary horizontal line.

The technique is false satin stitch. The leaves and outlines are worked in slanting satin stitch.

The pattern is an earlier variety of the design used for the decoration of the sheet borders under Cat. Nos. 1955.516 (Fig. 40) and T.1970.2 (Fig. 38).

Formerly in the collection of the Wolfner family.

Made in Northern Hungary, mid-17th century.

Length: 73 cm. Width: 22.5 cm. Cat. No.: 1955.400.

40 Sheet border

Whitework embroidery on fine linen.

The wide middle section has large pomegranates with serrated leaves and open, Baroque-style tulips in alternating orientation. The tulips have two lobed leaves issuing from the stem. The flowers are enclosed in medallions of four sprigs of serrated leaves. A ribbon ties them together at their meeting point. Small tulips issue from the leaf stalks. The two narrow bands show pomegranates. The shapes are filled with pearl-like French knots. The centre of the pomegranates, the petals of the tulips, and the veining of the large leaves are patterned by leaving portions of the fabric unstitched. The pattern is a variation on the embroidered end of pillow-slip Cat. No. 1955.400 (Fig. 39).

Northern Hungary, early 18th century.

Length: 160 cm. Width: 23 cm. Cat. No.: 1955.516.

41 Sheet border

Whitework cotton embroidery on white linen ground.

Every second square opening of the cutwork mesh is overcast with a cross-stitch. The principal motif consists of an S-shaped vine terminating at each end in a carnation. A rosette, with spurs, is placed in the middle of the vine, which also has a pair of small flowers and leaves. The central design is bordered on either side by a narrow festoon of rosettes, tulips, and pomegranates. The border is edged with an 11 cm wide white bobbin lace with ribbon motifs and scalloped edging. The cutwork embroidery is identical on both sides of the fabric. The patterns are in geometric satin stitch with the outlines in diagonal satin stitch. The centre of the rosettes is filled with lace stitch.

Formerly in the Wolfn er collection.

Northern Hungary, second half of the 17th century.

Length: 170 cm. Width: 43 cm, with lace: 54 cm. Cat. No.: 1955.498.

42–43 Tablecloth

Light red, blue, green, yellow silk and gold embroidery on fine white linen.

The narrow border shows a row of tulips placed within a semicircular spray of leaves. A second row of motifs consists of sprays of acanthus blossoms surmounted by a carnation. A spray of leaves branches off from the main stem to which it is joined by a ring. The composition of this floral group is enhanced by the broken arch of clustered tulips. The four corners are decorated with a diagonally set plant motif. Here, the centre stem ends in a peony blossom, while the two side stems bear carnations. Scattered sprays of tiny flowers and leaves complete the group. Animal figures between concentric floral garlands occupy the field of the cloth. A circle of daisies forms a medallion in the centre which encloses a stag and the initials F. K. The embroidery is identical on both sides of the cloth. The technique is very closely worked satin stitch.

Formerly in the possession of the Bánffy family.

Transylvania, mid–17th century.

Length: 234 cm. Width: 186 cm. Cat. No.: 1954.648.

44 ALTAR-CLOTH

Embroidered with dark red silk and silver threads.

The cloth is sewn together from two pieces of fine white linen. All four sides are decorated with flower and leaf motifs. The leaves have serrated edges with berries between the lobes of the outer edge. The central vein of the leaf is also serrated. From the base of the plant three stalks emerge bearing small pomegranates and a large peony blossom, the whole forming an oval with the curving leaf. The style reflects Persian and Italian Renaissance influences. The colour scheme and the stitchery vary with each motif.

Formerly in the Wolfner collection.

Transylvania, mid–17th century.

Length: 202 cm. Width: 71 cm. Cat. No.: 1955.387.

45 ALTAR-CLOTH

Fine white linen embroidered in light blue and green, and gold thread.

The long side of the cloth shows two rows of oval-shaped floral and foliar motifs. Small flowers grow between the lobes of each large, curling leaf, with a pomegranate motif at its base. The oval curve of the leaf enfolds a large carnation and a smaller flower. The alternate use of silk and gold thread creates a rhythmic colour effect.

Formerly in the possession of the Roman Catholic Church of Pécsújfalu.

Northern Hungary, mid–17th century.

Length: 224 cm. Width: 105 cm; width of embroidered border: 30 cm. Cat. No.: 1915.122.1.

46 EMBROIDERED STRIP

Fine white linen embroidered with rose pink, light blue, and light green silks and gold thread.

The large segmented pomegranates are set between lobed leaves and separated by garlands of tulips. Added features are small tulips and other floral forms. The silk and gold threads, worked in tiny satin stitch, give the embroidered surface a sparkling appearance. Some elements of the design have a zigzag pattern of *point de Hongrie* stitching.

Purchased by the museum from Fülöp László.

Northern Hungary, mid–17th century.

Length: 257 cm. Width: 27 cm. Cat. No.: 1904.82.2.

47 Sheet border

Thin white linen, embroidered in coloured silk and gold thread.

The sheet comes from the trousseau of Kata Bethlen, wife of Mihály Apafi II, Prince of Transylvania. The pattern shows carnation and tulips under an arcading vine scroll. Each stem in encircled by rings and rests on a pair of large, serrated leaves. The composition of the decorative elements is typical of Renaissance ornamentation. The shape of the leaves and the small pear-like fruits speak of oriental influence.

The embroidery is worked in *point de Hongrie* on the right and reverse sides. The satin stitches follow the contours of the motifs in a zigzag line, and produce a shaded effect.

Formerly in the collection of the Wolfner family.

Transylvania, third quarter of the 17th century.

Length: 144 cm. Width: 15 cm. Cat. No.: 1955.429.

48 Detail of embroidered alter frontal *(Antependium)*

Light pink, yellow, green, and two shades of blue silk embroidery on fine white linen.

The so-called Italian jug pattern shows two amphoras from which fifteen long-stemmed flowers issue. One vessel contains rosettes, two kinds of tulips, lilies, and carnations. The other holds rosettes, tulips, clustered berries, pomegranates, and two kinds of acanthus blossom. The remaining spaces are filled with a pattern of tulips, rosettes, acanthus sprays an other floral motifs. The blade-like and gracefully curling shapes of leaves soften the rigid lines of the upward curving stems. Atmost every species of flowers favoured by Hungarian embroiderers of the 17th century are represented. The technique is laid and couched work.

Formerly in the Wolfner collection.

Northern Hungary, second half of the 17th century.

Length: 83 cm. Width: 74 cm. Cat. No.: 1955.412.

49 Communion cloth

Fine lawn with gold and silver purl embroidery.

The four corners show a plant with two stems bearing pomegranates. Tendrils and small leaves run along the curving stems, and surround the fruits. The smaller stem of the corner motif is repeated in the middle of each side of the cloth. The overall composition and the design of the pomegranates display Turco-Persian influence. The tendrils, which relieve the rigidity of the design, are Gothic in style. The patterned satin stitch, filling the fruits, and the diagonal satin stitch, employed for stems and tendrils, are identical on both sides of the fabric.

Formerly in the Wolfner collection.

Northern Hungary, second half of the 16th century.

Dimensions: 101.5 × 101.5 cm. Cat. No.: 1955.376.

50 Communion cloth

Fine lawn with gold and silver embroidery.

Each corner is decorated with a bouquet in the shape of a rhombus. The central motif shows a stem bearing a tulip, a rosette, leaves, tendrils, and culminating in a pomegranate crowned with a small tulip. In the middle, the stem has two lateral shoots, each divided into two additional branches with carnation, rose, tulip and daisy motifs. The gracefully curving lines of the stems and the life-like drawing of the floral forms reflect the style of the Renaissance. Identical on right and reverse sides of the fabric, the embroidery is worked in patterned satin stitch.

Purchased by the museum from Jenő Endre.

Northern Hungary, mid-17th century.

Dimensions: 93×93 cm. Cat. No.: 1941.21.5.

51–52 CHALICE VEIL

Fine lawn embroidered with light red, blue, light green, pink, and cream silk, and gold and silver thread.

Each corner is decorated with a bouquet of flowers and stylized roots. The central stem bears a carnation, five-petalled tulips and leaves. Two entwined smaller stems bear a lily, a cluster of grapes, tulips, berries, pomegranates, buds, leaves and tendrils. The four lower stems bear four-petalled flowers, tiny tulips, leaves and tendrils. The design of opposite corners is identical, but neighbouring corners show slight differences in the pattern. The middle of two sides are embroidered with the Tree of Knowledge under whose flowering branches stand Adam and Eve and a running stag. The two other sides show the seated figure of the Madonna between flowering branches. In the centre of the cloth, enclosed in a medallion of leaves, is the *Agnus Dei*. The letters P. A. D. and the date 1651 are inscribed on the outside of the medallion. The heart-shaped design of the bouquets suggests that originally the veil was a betrothal kerchief. The kerchief may have been donated to the church after the wedding when the figures, letters and date were added. The embroidery, identical on right and reverse sides of the cloth, is worked in slanting satin stitch.

Formerly in the Wolfner collection.

Northern Hungary, 1651.

Length: 65 cm. Width: 62 cm. Cat. No.: 1955.386.

53 COMMUNION CLOTH

Dark red silk and gold purl embroidery on fine lawn.

The four corners and the middle of each side show a carnation and other floral shapes, their common stems terminating in a coil. The centre of the cloth is ornamented with carnations, tulips, rosettes, leaves and tendrils on a circular vine. The needlework is identical on right and reverse sides, and the motifs are worked in geometric satin stitch. The red and gold threads are applied alternately. The edging is gold bobbin lace.

Formerly in the Wolfner collection.

Northern Hungary, mid-17th century.

Length: 102 cm. Width: 100 cm. Cat. No.: 1955.389.

54 EMBROIDERY ON LADY'S COURT DRESS

The dress, which used to belong to Catherine of Brandenburg, wife of Gábor Bethlen, Prince of Transylvania, is embroidered with tulips, carnations and daisies in gold and silver thread.

The sumptuous decoration runs across the skirt in eight rows and is repeated on the sides and back of the bodice.

The work is patterned satin stitch.

Transylvania, 1625–29.
The band of embroidery on the skirt is 60 cm wide. Cat. No.: 1954.664.

VI, 55–56 CHASUBLE

Cherry red satin with gold and silver embroidery.

The field is divided lengthwise into three panels. The middle panel is covered with symmetrical flower motifs comprising carnations, acanthus blossoms, tulips and lilies of the valley. The two side panels have a scrolling vine pattern with leaves, pomegranates and carnations. The back of the vestment shows the arms of the Károlyi and Sennyey families. The front is inscribed with the date 1670. The embroidery is geometrical satin stitch. The chasuble was worked by László Károlyi and his wife Erzsébet Sennyey, and shows familiarity with Renaissance decorative techniques.

Purchased by the museum from the Ernst collection.

Transylvania, 1670.

Length: 128 cm. Width: 84 cm. Cat. No.: 1935.42.

VII–VIII, 57–58 COVERLET

Green and red silk velvet with gold and silver embroidery.

The coverlet is the work of Zsuzsanna Lorántffy, wife of György Rákóczi I, Prince of Transylvania. The green velvet field is covered with a pattern of floral sprays. The bouquet in each of the four corners is enclosed in a wreath of leaves suggesting the adaptation of Persian motifs to suit Renaissance taste. The bouquet with its three-stemmed floral spray reflects Italian influence. The centre of the field shows the armorial bearings of the principality of Transylvania enclosing the heart-shaped shield of the Lorántffy family. The entire motif is surrounded by a wreath of stylized leaves, echoing the theme of the corners. The red velvet border with its two kinds of floral forms and the scattered blossoms in the field display the characteristic Hungarian Renaissance blending of styles borrowed from the Orient and Western Europe. The embroidery is clearly the work of an accomplished embroideress who must have been well versed in the artistic idiom of the Renaissance. The technique is patterned satin stitch. The museum purchased the coverlet from the heirs of Tamás Erdődy with the help of a grant from the Ministry of Education.

Transylvania, second quarter of the 17th century.

Length: 200 cm. Width: 182 cm. Cat. No.: 1932.121.

59 CHASUBLE

Coloured silk embroidery on white twill silk shot with gold.

The pillar orphrey shows floral forms with carnations and the Louis XIV *baldachin* motif. The two side panels show curving vines with various flowers. The edging is of gold passementerie which is also used to separate the panels.

Purchased by the museum from the Piarists of Trencsén.

Hungarian, early 18th century.

Length: 118 cm. Width: 79 cm. Cat. No.: 1918.29.75.c.1.

60 HORSE-BLANKET

This blanket covered the horse's back behind the saddle. The field is covered with dense gold and silver embroidery. On a zigzag-patterned ground the decoration shows three palmettes topped with fan-shaped leaves. The motif in the middle is enclosed by two large leaves with serrated edges. On three sides the blanket has a border of alternating rosettes and lobed leaves. The borders are edges with rose pink satin decorated with fleurs-de-lis connected by an arcade of vines. The design reflects Turkish influence. The embroidery is geometrical couched work. Formerly in the possession of the Teleki family.

Transylvania, first half of 17th century.

Length: 122 cm. Width: 55 cm. Cat. No.: 1949.372.

61–62 SADDLE-CLOTH

Green broad-cloth with gold and silver embroidery.

Each corner is embellished by a floral spray with five stems. The leafy middle stem bears a carnation. Two lateral stems have pomegranates. Two spiralling outer stems terminate in pomegranates crowned by small tulips. Towards the back, one side of the cloth shows a similar plant motif in the middle. Here the design, however, is adapted to follow the horizontal line of the straight edge. The embroidery is geometrical couched work.

Formerly in the collection of the Bánffy family.

Transylvania, mid-17th century.

Length: 119 cm. Width: 114 cm. Cat. No.: 1958.26.

63–64 SADDLE-CLOTH

Green broad-cloth embroidered with gold and silver thread.

The two corners of the rear end show various floral forms and leaves. Between the corners a large carnation dissects the heart formed by two curling vines with flowers and leaves. Carnations decorate the two front corners. The technique is guimped geometric couched work.

Hungarian, second half of the 17th century.

Length: 114 cm. Width: 111 cm. Cat. No.: 1958.31.

65–66 WHITE LINEN NEEDLE-POINT LACE

The *punto in aria* technique is applied on a cutwork ground showing vine, floral, figural and bird motifs.

The lace was found among the discarded costumes of the Academy for Dramatic Art.

Venice, 16th century.

Length: 48.5 cm. Width: 3.3 cm. Cat. No.: 1954.629.

67 GOLD BOBBIN LACE

This specimen consists of two pieces of lace sewn together, an insert and a border with serrated leaf edge. It was made by knotting, which was the earliest form of the bobbin-made variety.

Found in the crypt of the Calvinist church of Losonc, in 1851.

Hungarian, late 16th century.

Length: 190 cm. Width: 14 cm. Cat. No.: 1853.5.B.26.

68 GOLD BOBBIN LACE

The net ground is worked with five-petalled tulips and other tulip motifs. The scalloped edge is bordered with picot.
Hungarian, early 18th century.
Length: 156 cm. Width: 25 cm. Cat. No.: T.1969.8.

69 EMBROIDERED SHEET

Linen with cutwork embroidery and bobbin lace on a network ground. The lace insert is decorated with palmettes. The lace edging shows pomegranates and vine leaves.
Hungarian, late 17th century.
Length: 310 cm. Width: 192 cm. Cat. No.: T.1963.4.

70 WHITE LINEN BOBBIN LACE

The repeating pattern consists of hearts surmounted by crosses, leaves and tulips on a *guipure* ground. It served originally as the border of an altar-cloth.
Hungarian, *c.* 1700.
Length: 172 cm. Width: 36 cm. Cat. No.: 1955.574.

71 WHITE LINEN BOBBIN LACE

On a *guipure* ground the lace has an irregular all over pattern. One side is edged with an openwork insert, the other has an edging of rounded and pointed scallops.
Hungarian, early 18th century.
Length: 137.5 cm. Width: 23 cm. Cat. No.: 1955.573.

72 WHITE LINEN BOBBIN LACE

The pattern shows large and small floral and leaf motifs and pomegranates. On the bottom the edge is unevenly scalloped.
Originally it was the accessory of an alb.
Purchased by the museum from the bishopric of Szepes.
Brussels, *c.* 1700.
Length: 208 cm. Width: 62 cm. Cat. No.: 1915.69.16.

73 ALB

The hem and cuffs are decorated with needle-point lace. On a net ground the pattern shows baroque motifs, plants, floral garlands and leaves. The *point d'Alençon* lace is worked with a variety of lace stitches. Purchased by the museum from the bishopric of Szepes.
French, 18th century.
Length of lace: 153 cm. Width: 74 cm. Cat. No.: 1915.69.13.

74 NETWORK LACE

Made of white linen thread, this was originally the edging of an altar-cloth.
The pattern shows a vase of flowers in the centre with the mirror images of St. George killing the dragon. One of the inscriptions reads: "Magarosi Anna", the other: *"Christus Urunk Peldaja Szet Gyory R Anno. Domini 1660"* (Mirror of our Lord Jesus Christ, St. George, A. D. 1660).
Hungarian, 1660.
Length: 150 cm. Width: 72 cm. Cat. No.: 1922.55.

75 RUG

Small Ushak, knotted in woollen pile.
The colour of the field is red with a blue hexagonal medallion of leaf and vine motifs and arabesques in the centre and braiding in the corners. The border has floral forms and vines on a blue ground.
Formerly in the Franciscan convent of Csíksomlyó.
Asia Minor, second half of 16th century.
Length: 157 cm. Width: 110 cm. Cat. No.: 1914.94.10.

76 KNOTTED WOOLLEN RUG

The red field shows arabesques in yellow. The border has a blue foundation on which motifs reminiscent of the Kufic alphabet appear with carnations, palmettes and stars.
Asia Minor, first half of 17th century.
Length: 184 cm. Width: 121 cm. Cat. No.: 1952.278.

77 RUG

Known as Transylvanian, knotted in woollen pile.
Flowering vines, issuing from two vases, cover the red field. The corners are deep blue with a pattern of rosettes and leaves. The yellow border, with elongated medallions in yellow and red, has an arabesque design with claws.
Purchased by the museum from the bishopric of Szepes.
Asia Minor, second half of the 17th century.
Length: 172 cm. Width: 133 cm. Cat. No.: 1915.69.10.

78 RUG

Known as Transylvanian, knotted in woollen pile.
The main pattern consists of a large cartouche of narcissus flowers and rosettes in the centre of a red field. Within the cartouche there are vases and floral motifs. The white border shows rosettes and in leaves various colours. Purchased by the museum from the bishopric of Szepes.
Asia Minor, 17th century.
Length: 167 cm. Width: 125 cm. Cat. No.: 1915.69.6.

79 RUG

Knotted in woollen pile.
The inner field is blue with a plant motif reminiscent of Hungarian Renaissance embroidery. Above it, in a horizontal band, are the letters D.S. and the date 1723. The border shows a repeating pattern of two-armed arabesques, elongated medallions and stars.
Woven in Transylvania, the design was inspired by rugs made in Asia Minor.
Transylvania, 1723.
Length: 120 cm. Width: 170 cm. Cat. No.: 1953.441.

LIST OF PLACE NAMES

Bajcs   – Bajč, Czechoslovakia
Bártfa   – Bardejov, Czechoslovakia
Besztercebánya   – Banská Býstrica, Czechoslovakia
Brassó   – Braşov, Rumania
Csíksomlyó   – Şumuleu, Rumania
Galgóc   – Hlohovec, Czechoslovakia
Gyulafehérvár   – Alba Iulia, Rumania
Kassa   – Košice, Czechoslovakia
Kisszeben   – Sabinov, Czechoslovakia
Kolozsmonostor   – Cluj-Mănăştur, Rumania
Losonc   – Lučenec, Czechoslovakia
Nagyszeben   – Sibiu, Rumania
Nagyszombat   – Trnava, Czechoslovakia
Nagyvárad   – Oradea, Rumania
Nyitra   – Nitra, Czechoslovakia
Olmütz   – Olomouc, Czechoslovakia
Pozsony   – Bratislava, Czechoslovakia
Selmecbánya   – Banská Štiavnica, Czechoslovakia
Sztropkó   – Stropkov, Czechoslovakia
Torda   – Turda, Rumania
Trencsén   – Trenčin, Czechoslovakia
Valpó   – Valpovo, Yugoslavia

PLATES

I St. John. The embroidered figure is on the chasuble shown in Figs. 1 and 2. *c*. 1400

III The arms of King Matthias. Detail of throne dossal (Fig. 19). Florence, *c.* 1470

IV Embroidered corner motif of pillow-slip (Fig. 28). Hungarian, *c.* 1650

V Embroidered sheet (Fig. 29). Transylvania, mid-17th century

VI Detail of embroidered chasuble (Fig. 55). Transylvania, 1670

VII The arms of Transylvania and the Lorántffy family on a coverlet (Figs. 57–58). Transylvania, second quarter of 17th century

VIII Embroidery on the border of a coverlet (Figs. 57–58). Transylvania, second quarter of 17th century

1 Chasuble. Venetian velvet brocade with Hungarian embroidery, c. 1400

2 Detail showing embroidered orphrey of chasuble in Fig. 1

4 Chasuble. Venetian velvet brocade, second half of 15th century. Northern Hungarian embroidery, second quarter of 15th century

◁ 3 Detail of chasuble. The embroidery is South German–Northern Hungarian, *c.* 1400

6 Chasuble. Venetian velvet brocade, first half of 15th century. Hungarian embroidery, mid-15th century

◁ 5 Cross of a chasuble with Hungarian embroidery, mid-15th century

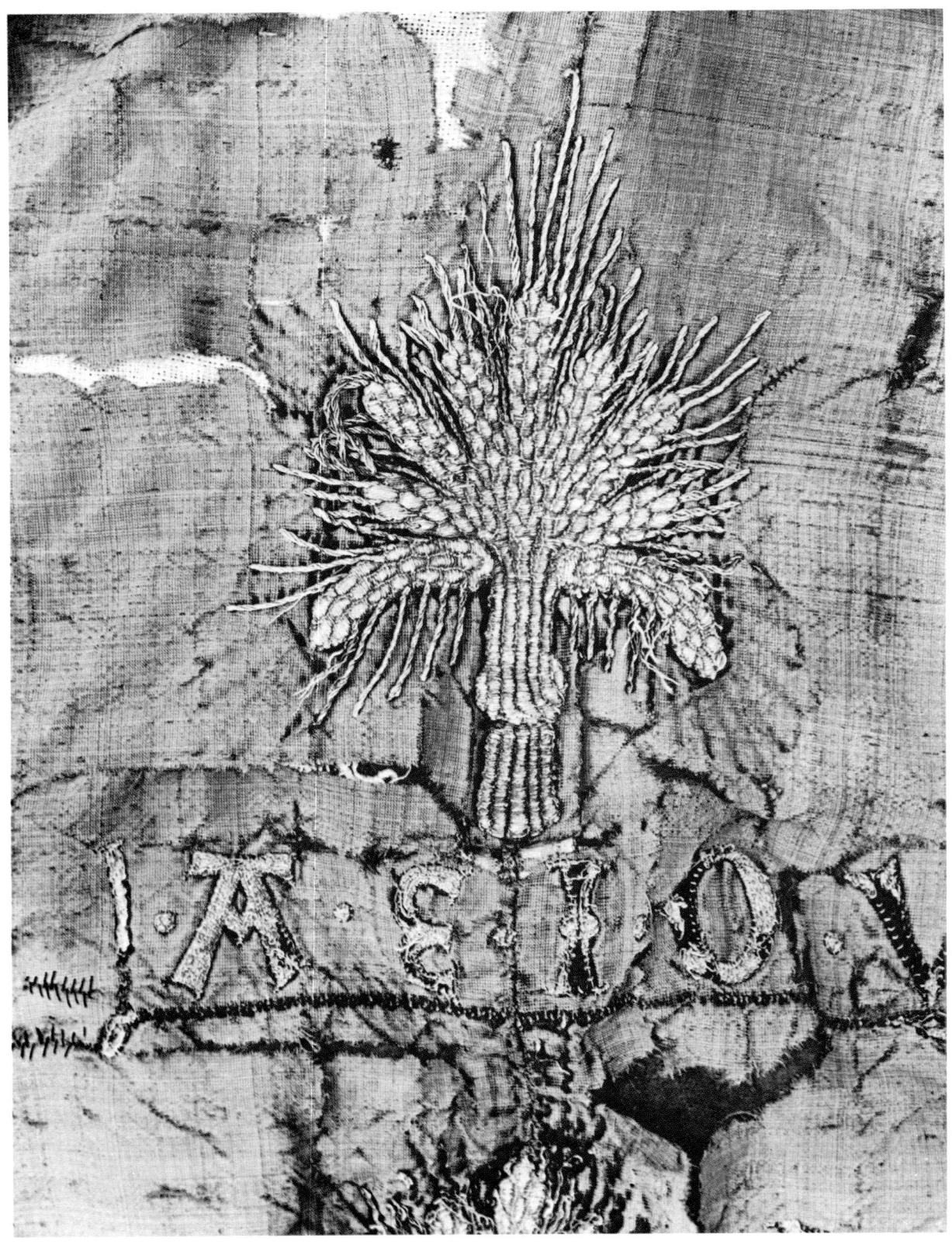

7 Pluvial with wheat-sheaf embroidery, 1448

8 Shield of a pluvial. German, first half of 15th century

9 Chasuble. Florentine brocade, *c.* 1470. The embroidery is of Austrian–South German provenance, early 16th century

10 Chasuble. Florentine brocade, second half of 15th century, with Hungarian embroidery, late 15th century

12 Detail showing Hungarian
   embroidery on chasuble. Late 15th century

◁ 11 Detail showing Hungarian embroidery on chasuble.
   Late 15th century

13 Chasuble. Venetian brocade, second half of 15th century. Embroidered in Florence, 1470–80

14 Detail of chasuble in Fig. 13

15 Chasuble. Venetian brocade, last quarter of 15th century. Embroidered in Venice, *c.* 1470

16 Chasuble of Venetian velvet brocade with Italian embroidery, both *c.* 1500

18. Handwoven cloth with turrets and figural design. Hungarian, second half of 15th century

◁ 17 Cross of a chasuble. The *or nué* work is Italian, early 16th century

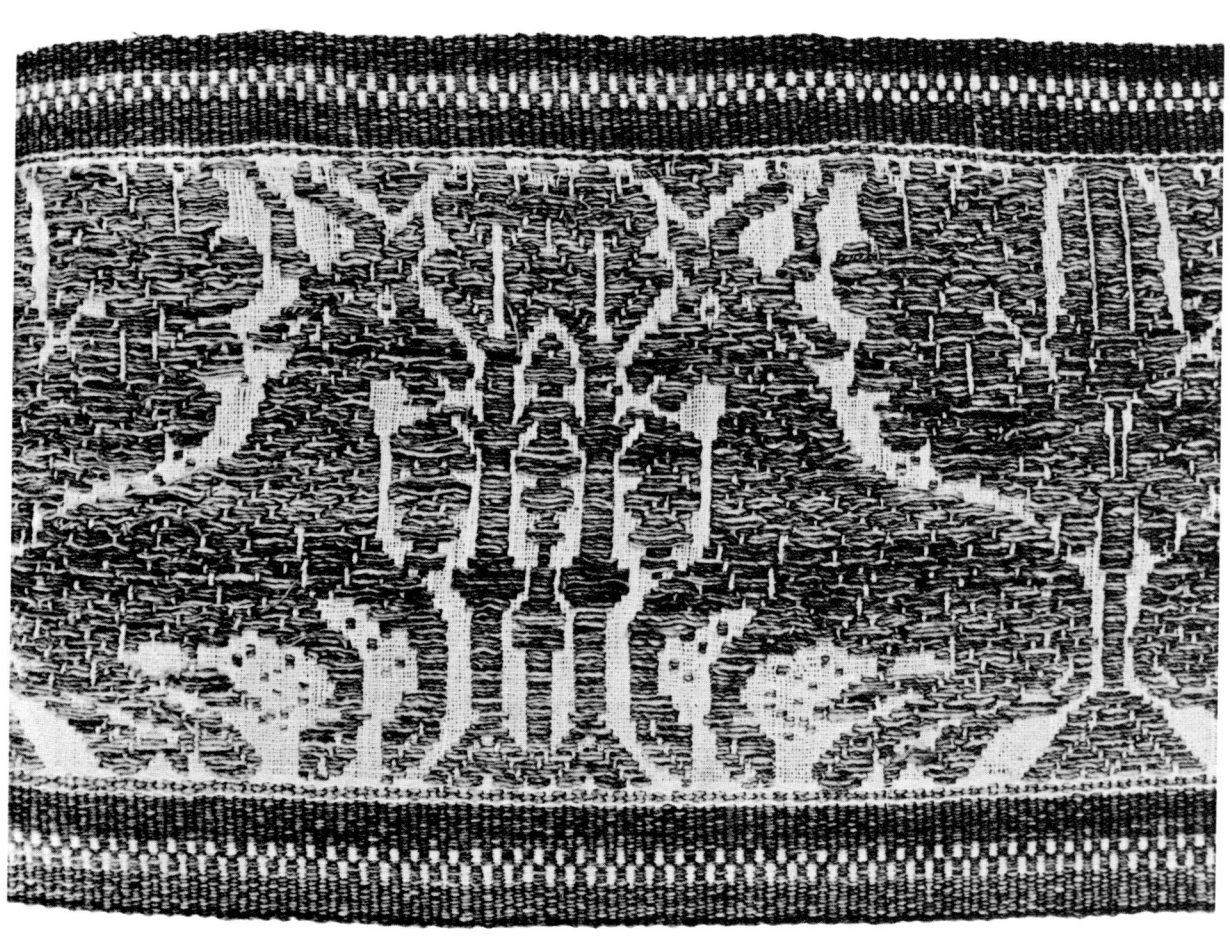

19 Pillow with woven animal motifs. Hungarian, first half of 16th century

20 Dossal of King Matthias's throne. Florentine gold brocade, c. 1470

21 Belt for a ceremonial sword. Italian gold brocade, 1509

22 Pillow-slip. Linen embroidered with tulips and vines. Transylvania, mid-17th century ▷

23 Embroidered end of a pillow-slip. Fine lawn with pomegranate and bow motifs. Northern Hungary, mid-17th century ▷

24 Pillow-slip. White taffeta with coloured silk, gold and silver embroidery. Transylvania, second half of 17th century ▷ ▷

25 Embroidered end of a pillow-slip. Linen, with pomegranates worked in dark red and gold thread. Transylvania, third quarter of 17th century ▷ ▷

26 Embroidered end of a pillow-slip. Cutwork embroidery on linen showing pomegranates in wreaths. Northern Hungary, second half of 17th century ▷ ▷ ▷

27 Pillow-slip. Embroidered linen showing floral motifs and vines in various colours. Transylvania, mid-17th century

28 Pillow-slip. Fine lawn with pineapples and floral motifs embroidered in coloured and gold thread. Hungarian, *c.* 1650

29 Sheet. Linen with plants embroidered in *point de Hongrie*. Transylvania, mid-17th century

30 Pillow-face. White-on-white embroidery on linen in knot stitch and openwork. Northern Hungary
mid-17th century

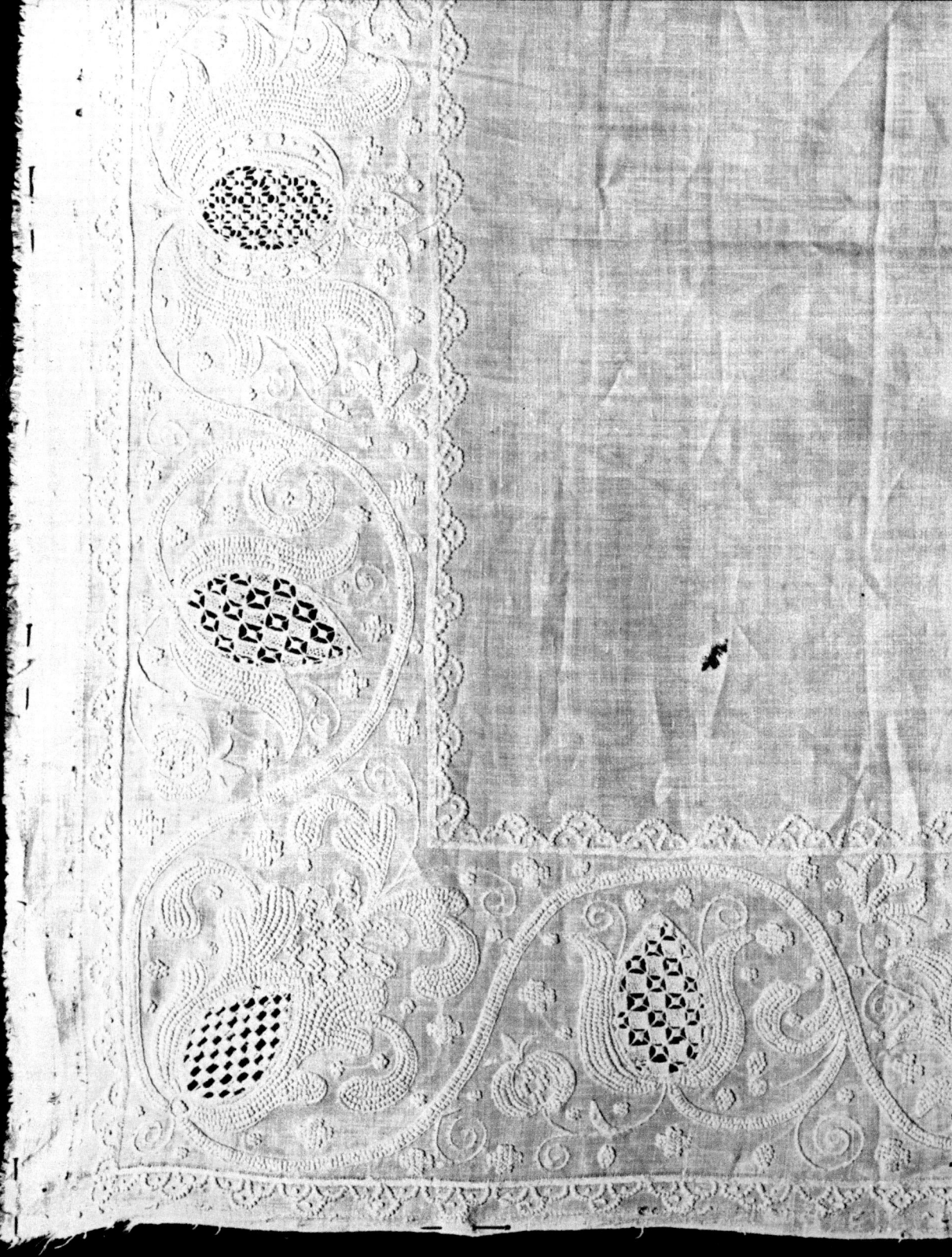

31 Sheet border, detail. Linen embroidered with green and silver flowers and vines. Transylvania, mid-17th century

32 Sheet border. Coloured silk and silver embroidery on linen. The pattern shows bouquets in a square composition.
Northern Hungary, third quarter of 17th century

33 Sheet border. Linen showing bouquets and leaves on an undulating vine in coloured silk and silver thread. Hungarian, mid-17th century

34–35 Sheet border. Linen, with white cutwork embroidery of flowers and vines. Northern Hungary, third quarter of 17th century

38 Sheet border. Fine lawn, with gold and silver embroidery. The pattern shows flowers within garlands of leaves. Hungarian, early 18th century

◁ 36 Sheet border. Whitework embroidery on linen, trimmed with bobbin lace. Northern Hungary, end of 17th century

◁ 37 Sheet border. Linen, with whitework embroidery showing large flowers on an undulating vine. Northern Hungary, third quarter of 17th century

39 Embroidered end of a pillow-slip. Linen, with rosettes surrounded by leaf-garlands. Northern Hungary, mid-17th century

42 Tablecloth. Linen, embroidered with coloured silk and gold thread. The pattern shows flowers and small animals. Transylvania, mid-17th century

43 Detail showing the corner motif of tablecloth in Fig. 42 ▷

◁ 40 Sheet border. Linen with whitework embroidery. The flowers and garlands of leaves are worked in knot stitch. Northern Hungary, early 18th century

◁ 41 Sheet border. Linen. The S-shaped vines are worked on a cutwork ground. The trimming is Hungarian bobbin lace. Northern Hungary, second half of 17th century

44 Altar-cloth. Linen. The row of flowers and lobed leaves are embroidered in deep scarlet and gold. Transylvania, mid-17th century

45 Altar-cloth. The embroidered floral motifs are worked in light blue, green and gold thread on linen ground. Northern Hungary, mid-17th century

46 Embroidered linen strip. The pomegranates under arcades of floral vines are worked in light coloured silk and gold thread. Northern Hungary, mid-17th century

48 Detail showing linen altar frontal embroidered in coloured silk thread. The pattern shows bouquets of flowers in amphoras. Northern Hungary, second half of 17th century ▷

49 Communion cloth. Fine lawn embroidered with pomegranates and stems in gold and silver thread. Northern Hungary, second half of 16th century ▷ ▷

50 Communion cloth. Gold and silver embroidery on fine lawn. Northern Hungary, mid-17th century ▷ ▷

51–52 Chalice veil and detail with the figures of Adam and Eve. Coloured silk, gold and silver embroidery on fine lawn. Northern Hungary, 1651 ▷ ▷ ▷

47 Sheet border. Linen embroidered with flowers worked in *point de Hongrie*. Transylvania, third quarter of 17th century

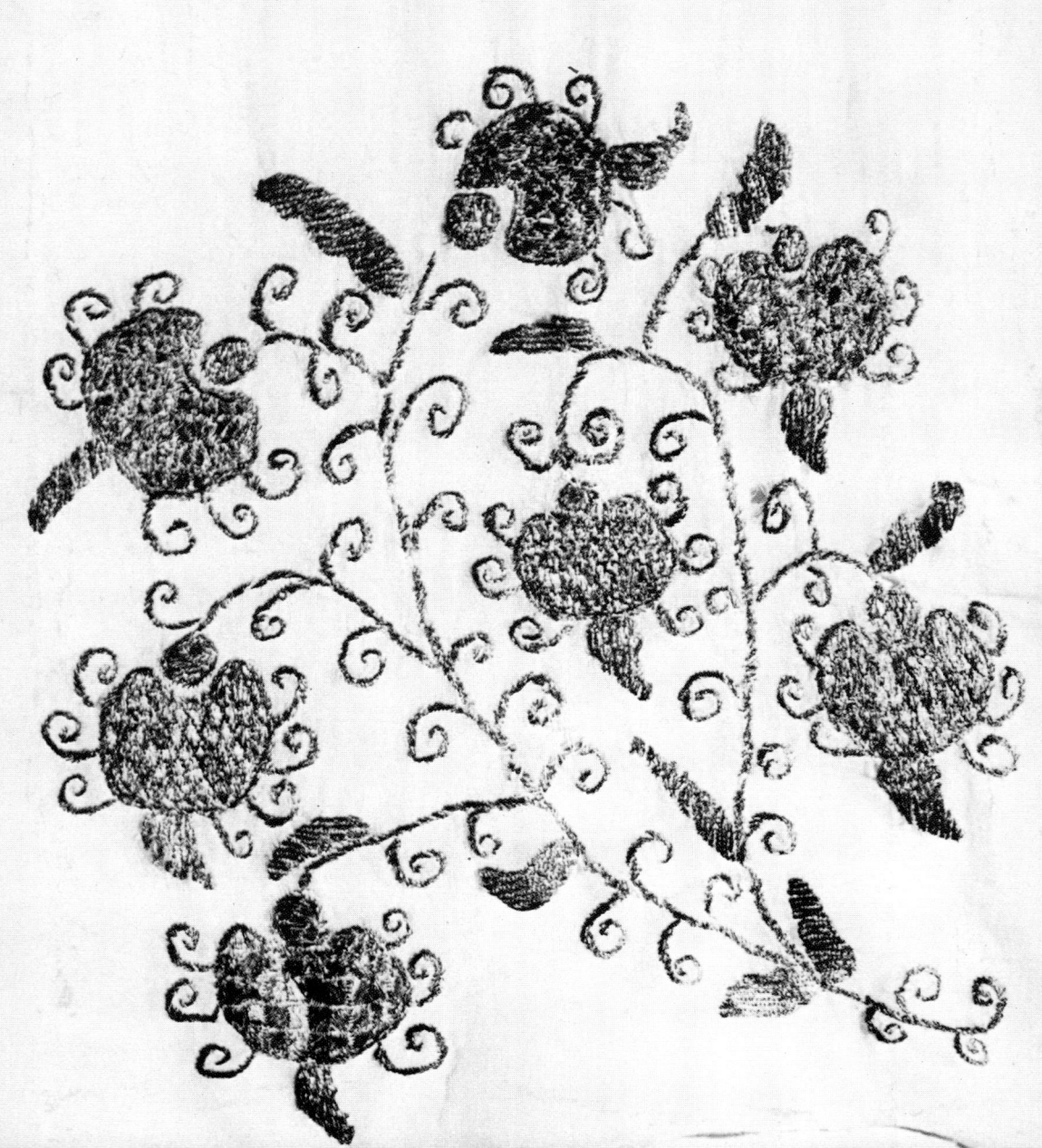

53 Communion cloth. Linen, embroidered in dark red silk and gold purl. Northern Hungary, mid-17th century

54 Detail showing lady's court dress embroidered with gold and silver thread. Transylvania, 1625–29

55–56 Chasuble. Red silk with gold and silver embroidery, showing the arms of the Károlyi and Sennyey families.
Transylvania, 1670

57–58 Coverlet. Green and red velvet with gold and silver embroidery. The arms are those of Transylvania and
the Lorántffy family. Transylvania, second quarter of 17th century ▷ ▷

59 Chasuble. White silk with coloured silk, gold and silver embroidery. Hungarian, early 18th century

60 Horse blanket with gold and silver embroidery. Transylvania, first half of 17th century

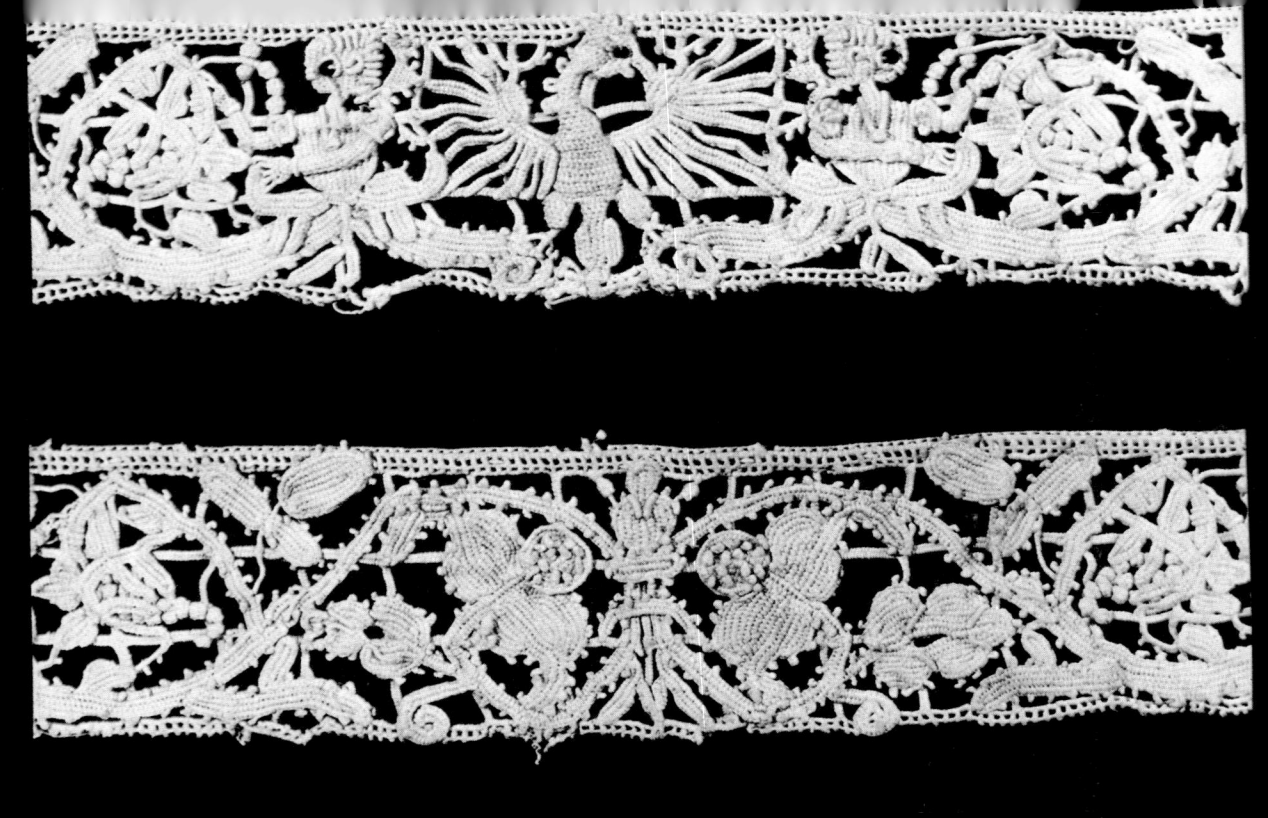

65–66 Needle-point lace. White linen. Venice, 16th century

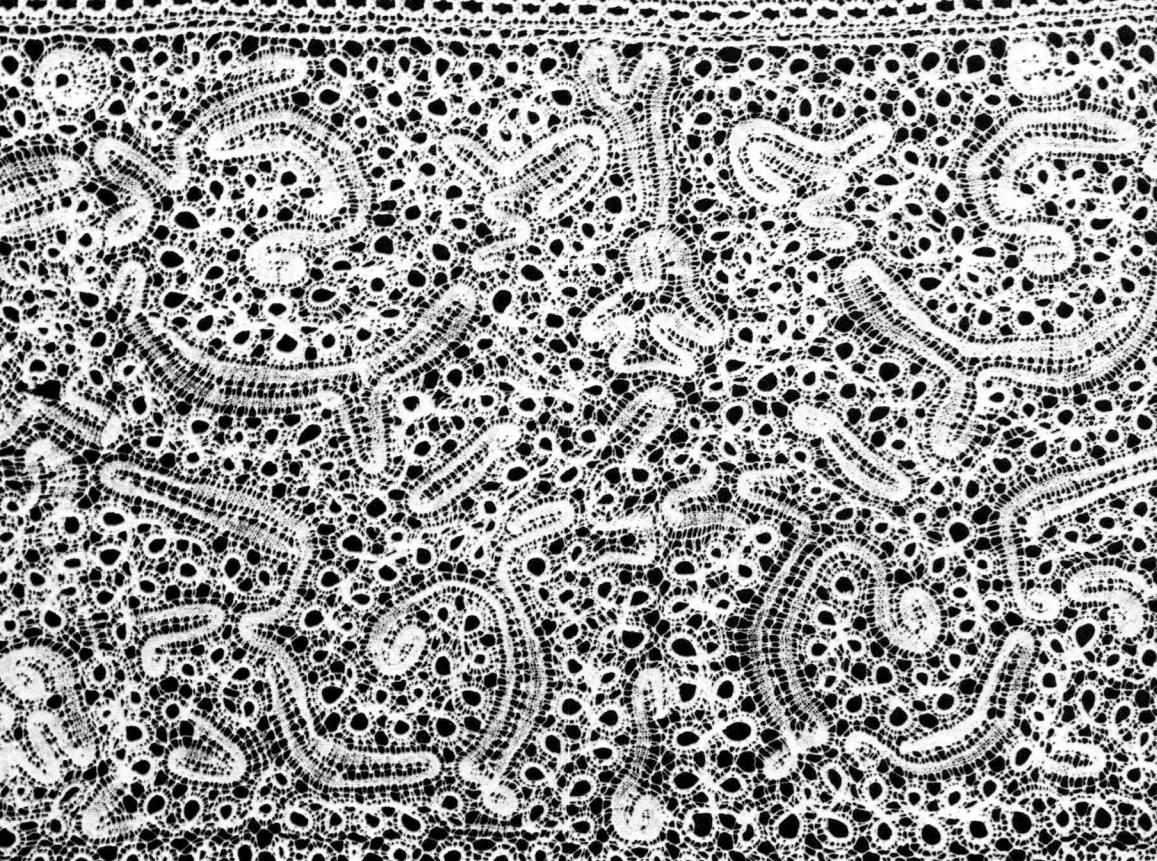

75 Rug. Small *Ushak*, knotted in woollen pile. Asia Minor, second half of 16th century

◁ 74 Linen network lace. The pattern shows St. George killing the dragon. Hungarian, 1660

76 Rug. Knotted in woollen pile and showing arabesque motifs. Asia Minor, first half of 17th century

77 Rug. So-called Transylvania rug, knotted in woollen pile. The pattern shows flowers and vines. Asia Minor, second half of 17th century

78 Rug. Knotted in woollen pile. This "Transylvania" rug has patterns of narcissus flowers in rosettes, and other floral motifs. Asia Minor, 17th century

79 Rug. Knotted in woollen pile. The field shows a bouquet and the borders have arabesques and stars.
Transylvania, 1723